THERE IS ANOTHER WAY

THERE IS ANOTHER WAY

Alternative and Therapeutic Education For Your Home-Taught Child

Radha Borthayre

authors
AND CO.

First published in Great Britain in 2024
by Authors & Co.
www.authorsandco.pub

ISBN 978-1-915771-94-0 (paperback)

CONTENTS

1. What Is Therapeutic Education? 1
2. Steps to Success 12
3. Learn to Trust and Heal – Dealing With Educational Trauma 26
4. Unleashing Potential – Is there a "Best" Way to Learn? 45
5. Unlearning the Labels – Embracing Growth Over Grades 58
6. Igniting Curiosity 72
7. Reluctance to Learning 88
8. The Art of Relaxation 97
9. The Problem and the Solution 104

About the Author 115

CHAPTER ONE

WHAT IS THERAPEUTIC EDUCATION?

What do the words "mainstream education" mean to you?

While "traditional" education often prioritises knowledge, transmission and the acquisition of specific skills, it typically follows a set curriculum delivered in a classroom setting. The primary focus is on mastering the subject matter and achieving pre-defined learning objectives, which are often assessed. There is little importance placed on self-management or emotional/social aspects.

This behaviourist approach is what most of us think of when we think about mainstream education.

Built on the idea that all behaviour is learned through interaction with the environment, a behaviourist approach emphasises observable behaviours. It is centred around the educator and uses techniques from operant and classical conditioning as a means of getting the learner to conform and learn. Allegedly, it was what the seventies song "Another Brick in the Wall" referred to.

A behaviourist approach, however, is not for everybody. One size does not fit all, and this has been a topic of conversation for a long time now. The education landscape is changing and many people are now questioning the system.

More and more children are finding it difficult to access a behaviourist approach. Families are turning away from mainstream education altogether. Whilst a lot of families may home-educate because they simply do not agree with the education system as it currently is, many families find themselves home-educating because they have no other option.

There are tens of thousands of children in the UK who are currently out of education, waiting for an alternative provision. An alternative provision is some form of education that is different to the current mainstream offering. It often requires specialist staff and a different approach to learning – an approach that meets their needs. As you can imagine, these are in short supply and the need is high, so, home-education might be the only provision available.

Children struggle in school for all kinds of reasons. Sometimes this is down to special educational needs and a lack of understanding (or time/ resource to implement any kind of support) from the school. Imagine a child with an invisible disability. Often, these children will be sanctioned for poor behaviour. They may be isolated and become known as the "problem child" in the class because of something they cannot control. Often these are the children that have to sit in the corridor to work or be separated from their peers. They are sometimes seen as the "naughty" one, and the stigma follows them around the school.

This can lead them down a path of destruction, which escalates to things like school suspension, exclusions, absences, etc., as the sanctions become more serious (all while missing the point of why the behaviour was happening in the first place). This then manifests itself in mental health issues for the child. Depression, anxiety, fear and meltdowns are some of the emotions that are present with school-based trauma in children. There is a process that they can go through to help recover from this, which we will talk about later, but how much better would it be if they didn't have to experience this trauma in the first place?

Eventually, for many people in this situation, school places will break down or the parent has to remove the child because the situation has become so bad. This is often a difficult time for the family and is when the real problems begin. They are now faced with a situation where their child is struggling to access any part of their life. There is no alternative provision in place and so, they have to find one for them. They may even face fines because their child is not attending school.

There may be other things at play, like fighting for an EHCP, asking the local authority to provide some form of education for their child while they are waiting for a placement somewhere, or even being asked to provide evidence of learning from home from the outset.

All these processes can be tiring, frustrating and expensive to go through. They can take years and often, the journey becomes one the entire family goes through.

The good news is that there are alternative options for education, and trauma can be recovered from. THERE IS ANOTHER WAY. The mainstream education model is the widest used form of education in the UK but it is by no means the only way to educate a child. In fact, there are PLENTY of alternative approaches that can be used if needed (or desired). This book will go through some of the different philosophies that underpin them, which will enable you to match these approaches up to individual children and their specific needs/interests.

Of course, it is not just the philosophies used in education that are important. It is also about looking holistically at every child and considering all their needs, not just their educational ones. It is about looking at the "Why" whenever certain behaviours are displayed, rather than dealing with the "What". This is what therapeutic education is. It is still the same academic content but also addresses the social, emotional and mental health needs of the learner at the moment in which they need it (real-time).

Do you ever feel, as an adult, that your weakest areas come from something that stemmed from your childhood and, even more specifically, something from school? Fear of failure, for example, may come from a situation that you were in years ago, that you never quite learned how to deal with – so much so, that you are still practising now as an adult. Let's talk about how we can help our children overcome some of the adversity that they may have faced already and use it as fuel for their future success going forward.

A THERAPEUTIC APPROACH TO EDUCATION

So, why are therapeutic education and alternative approaches to education important? Understanding the learning needs of the whole child, not just the academic aspects, creates an environment in which they feel safe enough to learn. Regardless of whether our brains are neurotypical or neurodivergent, we have all been "the child" at some point. Think how much more confident, emotionally intelligent and open to learning/change we would be if we were supported with our feelings, strategies for anxiety and our mental health from a very young age.

Therapeutic education offers a unique approach that addresses both learning and emotional well-being.

It is a common misconception that therapeutic education is less focused on academic knowledge within clear subject disciplines because there is an emphasis on feelings, emotions and mental health. The point that is missed is that emotional intelligence is also something that needs to be learnt! It is a practice that we can only perfect by developing strategies when real life things actually happen. The two (academic and therapeutic education) are perfectly capable of running hand-in-hand. I would go as far as saying that they have to run hand-in-hand to get the best out of the child. Mainstream education is for the most part a behaviourist model. This means that only behaviours that can be observed are dealt with. Anything that cannot be seen is less important (i.e. feelings, attitudes).

Of course, the academic learning topics themselves are still important. The difference is that small tweaks in the overall strategy addresses the emotional side as well. This is what it means to teach the whole child. As an adult, if you have ever been in a situation where you feel socially awkward, or anxious, it is probably because you have not yet had the tools to deal with that sort of situation (although you might have learnt the logistics of that situation). For example going to a party you are invited to, but not knowing what to say to people or how to interact in situations you find yourself in when you get there.

It is worth noting here that to be "therapeutic" is not just a process or treatment to be reserved for those with social, emotional or mental health problems. Everybody has mental health; it's a state of mind that alters throughout our lives as a result of ever-changing life events. It is commonly only spoken about though when things start to go wrong.

A therapeutic approach to education is about nurturing mental and emotional health right from the beginning before anything actually goes wrong. It is a more preventative approach. Is it not the case that we have the capacity to be so much more academically able if we are not being held back by our mental health or emotional issues?

Although it does not have to be used exclusively (though it is possible, it is better for the child if multiple approaches are adopted at the same time), a therapeutic approach is important to incorporate into any educational approach. In this book, we will explore different approaches to learning and how they can be used together to formulate the perfect recipes for different children.

Therapeutic education can and should complement traditional education by focusing on the "how" and "why" behind the behaviour during the learning process, ultimately empowering individuals to take control of their well-being and achieve their full potential within that learning process. It's the missing link in the National Curriculum – a crucial factor that has been missed all along.

NEURODIVERSITY IN THE MAINSTREAM EDUCATION SYSTEM

On one hand, we see neurodiversity for what it is. We have begun to place more importance on mental health than ever before, we understand strategies for learning and we have a deeper appreciation for the fact that we all learn differently and that our SEMH (social, emotional and mental health) needs are just as important as our academic intelligence.

On the other hand, when we get into the nitty gritty of things like attendance, or school refusal, we are still not looking deep enough into why the issues are arising. The attitudes of the institution are still very much just to get children through those school gates at any cost, as though that, in itself, will educate them and is the best place for them.

The problem with this scenario is, that if a child suffers from anxiety or has a legitimate reason why they struggle to attend, they will never be able to access learning by being forced through the school gates. They will spend their entire time in school in "fight or flight". The therapeutic element has been completely missed.

There are countless scenarios where pupils are reprimanded for "behavioural problems". The entire school staff knows who they are – they are the ones that the teachers complain about in the staffroom. Without realising it, the teachers themselves are indoctrinated into a system in which behaviourism is the only approach they know. I know this because *I was one of them,* and it was an emotional process to unlearn a lot of what I had been taught in my initial teacher training.

As a teacher, the "go to" option when a child did not display desired behaviour was to come up with an appropriate sanction (following the school's behaviour policy). I don't know if it was because I was new in the profession and inexperienced back then, but for a long time, it never occurred to me – or many of my colleagues – to look deeper. Buzzwords would fly around amongst the staff and I would hear things like, "This student has autism, so will need intervention". Back then, I believed this to mean that a teaching assistant would come in and support the student sometimes, or I would need to split something down into smaller chunks and they would be able to magically access it. In my mind, that was the extent of what autism support looked like and everything else was just bad behaviour.

It is important to note here that this is not the fault of the teacher. Without sounding defensive, we were never taught to look at the root of the behaviour. I didn't even know that there was more to it or that the tools to understand or deal with that ASD student therapeutically even existed. Even now, most schools adopt a behaviourist approach, with a designated SENCO – one member of staff in an entire school that has training on a bit more than just neurotypical learners and a sequential curriculum. Even then, the focus is on providing a temporary solution in a separate part of the school building for a struggling child before re-integrating them back into a mainstream classroom, as though they will magically be cured of their inability to conform by being isolated for a bit, then thrown back in. This is commonly a path that leads to things like missing school, exclusions and other behavioural consequences set out by school policies.

There is a clear indication here that from the top down, there is a gap in training for new teachers and there is an indication that the system itself needs more than just a sequential curriculum and a behaviourist approach to teaching and learning. Furthermore, pastoral care and mental health services are not a bonus add-on! It is a necessary tool and literally the difference between being able to access education or not for some. There should be as much focus on those as there is on academic education for learning to be a truly enriching experience for all children.

WE HAVE TO START ASKING QUESTIONS

What if it was never a behavioural problem to begin with? What If the child was presenting a particular behaviour to mask an emotion like fear or anxiety? Or a learning need because they couldn't access content in the way that it was being taught? What if the only tool that the teacher had to deal with this pupil was a behavioural one and they were never taught to ask why and look deeper into what that child was trying to communicate?

Perhaps, eventually, that child would become excluded, or a long-term absent child. Maybe they would be forced to go to school and endure the trauma again and again because the underlying cause was not picked up using the school's behaviour policy. It sounds a little bit like trying to put a square peg in a round hole, doesn't it? And yet, it is what happens, day after day. So many children are unable to access mainstream schooling because nobody thought to check the shape of the hole. They are too busy simply trying to squeeze it in so that they can get on with the rest of the day.

Then, there are the other children who sit somewhere in the middle of this extreme, trying to access learning with all the usual pains that come with being a child or an adolescent.

To help visualise the additional benefit that a therapeutic approach can provide, think of mainstream education as providing a toolbox. It equips you with general tools (knowledge and skills) but doesn't necessarily teach you how to apply them in your specific situation. Therapeutic education, on the other hand, helps you identify the tools you need, teaches you how to use them effectively for your unique challenges and fosters a sense of confidence in your ability to manage your situation.

Children haven't changed since the 1980s and 1990s but as a nation, many of us have become more aware and ready to talk about mental health, even more so since the pandemic. Cultures and attitudes towards education and life have changed and there is definitely more call for a holistic approach.

Accordion to leading mental health charity, Mind, In the UK, mental health concerns are widespread, with roughly one in four people experiencing a mental health problem each year[1]. This translates to one in six people in England reporting symptoms of common issues like anxiety and depression in any given week. While the overall number of individuals with mental health conditions hasn't significantly changed in recent years, the prevalence among children and young people has seen a concerning rise.

What about the judicial system?

The statistics shown on www.gov.uk suggest that a third of young offenders who are convicted or sentenced are neuro-divergent.

According to another source, JusticeInspectorate.gov.uk:

- About one and six people in the mainstream population are thought to be neurodivergent.
- One in four in the unemployed population is thought to be neurodivergent.
- At least one in three people moving through the justice system are neurodivergent. Many will have not been diagnosed during school.

1. https://www.mind.org.uk/information-support/types-of-mental-health-problems/mental-health-facts-and-statistics/

This begs the question, could we really reduce the number of young offenders by as much as 30% if we supported neurodivergent learners better in school or through their young lives? Is it not time that we started to look for another way? A better way?

CHAPTER TWO

STEPS TO SUCCESS

After thirteen years, I'd had enough. Having taught in four secondary/sixth form schools across the Midlands, I was fortunate enough to see a plethora of different ways of working within education – from 2000-pupil mainstream schools with sixth-form colleges attached, to small, specialist provisions for students with special needs. As a passionate teacher and ambitious woman who wanted to make an impact, I had diligently worked my way up the career ladder over the years. I planned to be a headteacher of one of these schools one day and retire happy.

Things didn't exactly work out that way.

It became more and more apparent to me as my career progressed that there were some real holes in the mainstream education model and they were simply not being filled – large class groups, a lack of training and support for SEN, stressful workplaces where everyone was feeling pressure on different levels and ridiculous workloads were just a few.

Three of the schools I worked in were inner city mainstream schools. The last one was the one I stayed in the longest and it was the most challenging (but rewarding) of all. It was an SEMH school, an alternative provision for children with social, emotional and mental health challenges. I say it was challenging not because the children were difficult, though they could be, but because it took me to the edge of my knowledge and tested every aspect of my practice further than anything I had ever experienced. It made me realise that in a job where I was trained and told I knew all the things I needed to know, the reality was that I knew very little. It made me question everything about every strategy I had ever learnt in my profession and push boundaries further to really be able to help the children that I met there.

Sometimes, this was as small as being a shoulder to cry on when they were having problems or wanted to talk or someone to listen. This was so because you are never just a teacher to them in a setting like that. You take on the role of parent, councillor, friendly face, role model, safe person and builder-upper of their entire world. I had to be a more active listener than ever before when they were trying to explain how they were feeling or some of the behaviours they were showing. It was something I had not really practised in mainstream education – to not immediately respond to behaviour but, instead, be on their side a bit more and try to look beyond it to see why it was happening and what that child was trying to communicate. This was one of the things that I learned: All behaviour is communication.

Most of the students I met back then were there because mainstream school placements had broken down.

If a child is reprimanded or disciplined when they have displayed a less-desirable behaviour (e.g., not sitting still when the teacher is speaking), that child may learn to "mask" the behaviour for fear of getting into trouble again. In other words, they hold it together and pretend like everything is okay until they are in a space safe enough to be able to let out all their emotions, then it all comes at once. Furthermore, such a reprimand takes away the child's ability to express what they were trying to communicate, which can lead to other negative behaviours down the line. It is this cycle I wanted to break.

As my experience continued to grow, I started to ask questions like, "What do these families need?" and "Why is nobody talking about it?" These questions swirled around and around in my head. I knew there had to be a better way to help these people.

Then came the magic.

I eventually left formal education and set up Little Crafters Boxes (and subsequently LCB Education) to help those who had fallen through the cracks and did not have any support yet. Some of my clients were home-educating, and others were waiting for a place in an alternative provision.

For the first time, all the pieces started to fit together and I finally created a concept that worked for thousands of families. It was (and is) truly amazing. I will talk about this more later.

HOW CAN A THERAPEUTIC APPROACH BE HELPFUL?

Three things to think about when considering any educational approach are:

Firstly, all the different philosophies of education have relevance and are important. You can't just pick one and say that is the only one that all children must follow. It will simply not work. We are all different.

Secondly, we need to consider the whole child (this is where a therapeutic approach comes in). Education without emotional support and consideration for mental health is a badly designed recipe. The two must go hand in hand for the whole thing to be truly successful. You wouldn't go on a treadmill at the gym and hop along it on only one foot, or read only one page in your favourite book, would you? You need both feet, and you would probably want to read the whole book!

Thirdly, the entire family/ wider dynamic is a very important cog in considering the approach to education for a child. Family wishes, their relationship with the child (and in the wider family), cultural differences, health issues, etc., will all have an impact on what they want/need for their child. It is important to approach this without judgement and from a place of wanting to help (and knowing the full picture of what is available in the education world) to be truly able to support the education of that child.

A therapeutic approach to learning takes all of this into account and puts the whole child at the centre of things.

Giving the child an opportunity to talk about things and really listening to them can be really valuable to gain insight into the bigger picture. Looking beyond the words they use and their body language and asking yourself where this behaviour came from can be helpful for them – and for you – to tackle it at its root. In doing so, we often find that behaviour can present itself from a place of emotion, e.g., anxiety, boredom or fear. It may be an undiagnosed SEN need. Other times, it might be covering up something more serious that can be missed entirely.

Here are some scenarios to illustrate what the behaviour might look like and how it may present itself. These are real scenarios taken from children I have worked with, with real struggles. The words are from the perspective of the parent (written in their words). All cases have been anonymised.

CASE ONE

> *"I started Home Ed after pulling my son from school. He has ADHD (plus suspected ASD) and he described school as prison. They had pulled him off me from the day he started nursery and that continued throughout primary school. They promised he would get support once he had his diagnosis. That support never happened. He was very rarely in class as the teacher couldn't handle his fidgeting, so very little learning was happening. I dreaded him coming home from school each day as the meltdowns were horrendous and it was me that he took it out on as I was the one who made him go to that prison!"*

This is a classic case of a SEN child, where the fidgeting behaviour is misunderstood by the teacher and mistaken for negative behaviour. It was dealt with in a way that made the child feel as though they were being punished for something they genuinely could not control, rather than finding strategies to support them. This resulted in isolation and eventual school refusal, which led to home education.

A more therapeutic approach in this scenario would have been to look at why the child was fidgeting, understand that there was potentially a special educational need there and try to find strategies to support the fidgeting, rather than to stop the child from doing it entirely. Something like a sensory toy, chair band, or standing desk (yes.. it is ok to stand up and learn as well as sit down and do so) might have alleviated the problem altogether.

CASE TWO

> *"We decided to deregister when L was told to just copy from the board and to "man up". Our biggest challenge was L's friends saying he was doing work they did more than two years ago. It leads to self-doubt and upset. L wanted to stop learning as he believed there would be no end result."*

In this scenario, there is a lack of motivation, initially, due to boredom in the classroom and potentially, it demonstrates a struggle to access the curriculum. This can happen if the content is too easy/ difficult, or not of interest. Negative wording from adults and other peers created self-doubt and a breakdown in confidence, which has then manifested in a reluctance to learn, with a belief that he can't achieve.

If we look exclusively at the behaviour, what we are seeing is defiance. If we look a little bit deeper with a therapeutic eye, we can observe that the initial behaviour was a lack of interest. There would have been a reason for that lack of interest. Was it the topic itself, the way in which it was being delivered or the challenge level? If the child was not engaging, then perhaps they needed a different strategy to absorb the information too? For a teacher to ask these questions would require them to look at their own practice as well as the needs of the child. Just to look at surface level behaviour will not deal with the issue in the long term.

This situation resulted in the breakdown of schooling as it escalated, and for the child, is now a fear of failure and school-based trauma. If we deal with those things and work on building confidence and resilience factors, the behaviour that we are trying to remove will start to repair itself.

CASE THREE

> *"My son has autism. He started refusing to go to school. Instead of supporting us, the school fined us! My daughter has anxiety. She was only in the first year of school but was so scared that she would be put in the corner that she wouldn't even ask to use the toilet."*

From a behaviourist perspective, we see defiance in this case. A child who is refusing to go to school gets sanctioned and the parent gets fined. Another child, who is accessing school is doing so in fear of consequences. She has been put in the corner where she will present the least possible problems for the teacher to be able to teach the class.

Let's look again at this from a therapeutic perspective. We now have a child who, for some reason, has struggled to access some part of school. If he has autism, this could be a variety of things, such as a struggle to access the sequential curriculum, sensory issues, crowds, social challenges or a combination of these. Figuring out what was causing the non-attendance and then attempting to fix that might have had a different result.

In the case of the girl, who is masking a lot of how she is feeling. This suggests she was not feeling safe enough to express herself in her environment. Her brain is in "fight or flight" mode, so she will not be able to use that part of her brain which can learn at this moment in time. Communication, smaller classroom environments and more interactions might have brought to light how she was feeling and helped to alleviate that so she could access learning.

MEDICATION

Medication was fairly commonplace in an alternative provision for students with SEN needs like ASD (autism) or ADHD (attention deficit hyperactivity disorder). Every morning and lunchtime, they would visit the school nurse to be given their medication. This would help them to regulate through the day.

For the most part, it was just accepted that that's the way it was and, in some cases, if a child was struggling day-to-day, they would be taken to the doctor to change their dose. There were conversations, from time to time, about alternative strategies to support regulation/sleep, and it was considered commonplace for medication to be grounds for debate on whether it was truly necessary or the correct route. Some children reported that medication worked well for them and others would flatly refuse to take it and said it created other issues for them.

Most of us think of medication as something we take that makes us better when we are sick. We don't think about the side effects and how they can affect us, day-to-day, if we have to continue to take it all the time. I remember a child once being spoken to for refusing to take his medication. He knew that not taking the medication would make him feel more hyperactive and unable to regulate himself. They were there to help him to calm down, which is what everybody around him wanted. But he said they also made him feel like a zombie. He couldn't taste food and his other emotions felt like they were dumbed down. He wanted to feel less hyperactive but he hated that he would then go through the rest of his day with these side-effects. That was his everyday dilemma. He wasn't trying to be "naughty".

WHAT TO DO WHEN EVERYTHING ELSE HAS FAILED

Start by taking a deep breath. It does not mean the children cannot be taught or are unable to learn. It means you have not quite matched them up to the strategy or the approach they need yet. The good news is that there are lots of strategies out there, and potentially thousands of things that you haven't tried yet. Tweak it a bit and keep going. You will eventually find something that works, and they will eventually start to engage. We are all predisposed to learn, after all. Humans have not changed that much over the years.

Something to note here is that if you are trying something that is not working, try not to keep doing the same thing again and again. Recognise that it is not working and try doing it a different way. Sometimes we can get stuck in the process, and all we really needed was a different angle.

Throughout my time at my final (SEMH) school, I quickly learned that traditional teaching strategies were not going to help children get through their GCSEs. I was a Computer Science teacher back then. It was a specialist subject which required prior knowledge in English and Maths and a real motivation to learn more. I had to learn and practice strategies to get disaffected children programming without using traditional academic learning strategies which simply would not work on this type of child. I didn't know if it had a name back then, but I do remember doing really "out there" things to spark their interests. I turned my classroom into a programmable haunted house, which would play spooky noises when you touched various things within the room.

Another time, we made fruit pianos, where the bananas represented keys on a keyboard, and they were all programmed by the children. The success I saw using this hands-on method was unreal. They loved the practical aspect. They were super engaged and wanted to share what they were learning with others. For the first time, I was able to teach curriculum topics, some of which had some rather challenging content, in this very practical way. It brought home to me the magic of practical learning – or, more specifically, the practice of learning therapeutically through play-based methods and whatever eco-friendly materials I had around me. Eventually, this became the very essence of the company I would go on to start – Little Crafters Boxes.

WHAT ARE THE STEPS TO SUCCESS?

If you have a child starting alternative education (this could be at home, or an alternative provision of sorts), the simplest steps to success are the same, regardless of whether the child is neurotypical or neurodivergent. Ask yourself why they did not enter the mainstream education system. What were the circumstances when they came out of it?

You do have other options and it is not that difficult once you know how. Don't rush into creating a school away from school, searching for the perfect alternative provision or putting lots of structure in again for them. The process will feel draining, and the amount of planning it requires is very intensive.

Talk to your child. Get to know them again in an educational capacity and assess where they are. Are they ready to learn yet? Do they have particular areas of interest? What approach to learning would suit their personality and might you be able to accommodate? If you encounter reluctance, deal with the reluctance first and be ready with strategies to help drive them (we will talk about this later).

If there is educational trauma, give them time to deal with this before moving on to formal learning. You cannot force learning when they are not ready to learn. It is important that they feel safe and nurtured in their environment before they can start to truly engage again.

Here are some secrets:

- It does not matter what "level" they are at or if they are working behind other children their age. They will catch up when they are ready. If they are not as good at something, the chances are, they are better than the average peer at something else
- They don't need to spend the entire day working! There is no right or wrong way to learn. Once you get on top of educating them at home, you will see that you can fit in a lot of learning in just a few hours.
- Let them play! It is how they are pre-programmed to learn. We are taught out of that at school in favour of formal learning in school but in some ways, that can do more harm than good. Learning through play is innate, and one of the best ways to learn.

This balance of academic learning, an alternative approach and placing importance on their mental health needs is therapeutic in every way, and the child will succeed. I have seen it, first-hand, with thousands of children.

STEPS TO SUCCESS FOR LITTLE CRAFTERS CHILDREN

My company, Little Crafters, Boxes has evolved since its debut back in 2021. It went from being a pandemic craft subscription box to offering a comprehensive package of learning resources for children of different ages and even adults. Over the years, I have watched the changing landscape in alternative education and, rather than riding waves with whatever the current trends were in the industry, I decided to take a different approach. I spent time listening to the children and their families and tweaked my company's offer accordingly.

Now I have a deep understanding of the community we service and Little Crafters Boxes, together with its child, LCB Education, provides everything from sustainable crafts and recognised accreditation to online lessons and project-based workbooks. This has made it a huge attraction for families who are home-educating or flexi-schooling. It has also started to attract local authorities, schools and groups who are using the Little Crafters Boxes' progressive way of learning. The transformations that we see with the children who work with us are unbelievable. The transformation from disengaged learners and children, with school-based trauma to individuals who take charge of their learning and can't get enough is a familiar sight within the community.

The best way to learn about children with additional needs is to work with them, get to know them and practise different strategies. I believe that the strategies one uses for children with additional needs are strategies that would work for all children. Therapeutic education provides more engagement, hands-on experiences and an opportunity to look deeper through natural curiosity.

AQA UNIT AWARD SCHEME

From my previous experience as a teacher and exams officer at an SEMH school, I knew I wanted to incorporate the Unit Award Scheme, brought about by one of the UK's largest awarding bodies, AQA. The Unit Award scheme provides an alternative way of learning for students who have struggled to access sequential learning and provides certification with a more interest-led approach.

Later down the line, when I became the CEO of a company championing families who needed support with home education, I approached AQA and persuaded them to let us trial the unit award scheme using a very progressive approach to learning. Nervously, they agreed to let us try it. It was a resounding success and LCB Education is now proudly one of the biggest providers of the scheme across the country.

I met with Adrienne Nichols, the Head of the Unit Award Scheme at the Festival of Education in 2024 and took the opportunity to interview her to find out more about it all.

> *"It is an achievement programme. Students receive certificates for achieving short units of learning, covering seventy curriculum subjects, some of which are covered in school but it also reaches much further than that. They cover everything from agriculture and horticulture right through to work-related learning and everything in between. As long as the unit provides a worthwhile and valid learning experience, it can be written into the scheme.*
>
> *UAS is designed to be used by children and adults of all ages. It has such versatility that the scheme can be adapted to meet the specific needs of a particular learner. It is great for those who might have struggled in a traditional classroom environment and perhaps been put off learning. It helps to coax them back by choosing interest-based topics and getting them to enjoy those learning experiences and then building up the programme of learning again to cover knowledge, learning and skills.*

It is about breaking the barriers to learning or the worry of an exam-based approach. There are no impending deadlines to meet and a "can do" attitude to learning, which can be recorded in any format.

The learner can spend time enjoying the learning experience and the teacher can spend time collecting evidence for the assessment part without the child needing to feel any anxiety about being tested."

— Adrienne Nichols, Head of UAS, AQA

WATCH:
AQA UAS interview with Adrienne Nichols
(Head of AQA Unit Award Scheme)

CHAPTER THREE

LEARN TO TRUST AND HEAL – DEALING WITH EDUCATIONAL TRAUMA

WHAT IS EDUCATIONAL TRAUMA? WHY DOES IT OCCUR?

Educational trauma is an emotional response to something that has occurred in school. This could be something physical that has happened to the child, such as bullying, witnessing/experiencing violence or social exclusion. It could also be academic pressure/underperforming or a teacher-student conflict, which leads to mistrust and feeling unsupported.

Like other traumas, it can be profoundly damaging to self-esteem, confidence and motivation. Often, it can lead to heightened negative emotions or even school avoidance/refusal. Children who go through school trauma need time to heal from the trauma before they can engage effectively with learning again. The mainstream schooling system does not always have support mechanisms in place for this, which is why many children end up in a situation where they need an alternative provision or need to be home-educated.

It is important to understand where the trauma comes from; what were the events that led up to it? Some children will be open to talking about this with a trusted adult or therapist. Others may struggle to be vocal about this for a while to come. It is common for children who have experienced trauma to withdraw or disengage from education or similar activities which lead up to the trauma until they have had time to process it.

Many children who become disengaged from learning or face permanent exclusion from school have fallen under the radar of the mainstream education system. It may be that they sit quietly in the room and therefore, it is assumed that they are paying attention to learning. They may be masking where they really are to give the appearance of understanding/learning/behaving so they can fit in and stay out of trouble. Other times, they may be doing the opposite and causing disruption in class, misbehaving and displaying negative behaviour. This can sometimes be a distraction to stop all the others from learning too so that they don't stick out as the one who didn't understand.

Often, behavioural challenges lead to sanctions and isolation. This can escalate to negative conversations with parents, suspensions and, eventually, school exclusion. There are rarely enough resources in the education system as it currently is to explore therapeutically why it all went wrong. Nor are teachers trained to recognise or try to understand the source of the "bad" behaviour.

One of the things that is important to understand is that all behaviour is communication. Also, attention is attention – if a child seeking attention is unable to get this positively, they will unconsciously start to seek this attention negatively. In a behaviourist system, this would lead to sanctions and disciplinary strategies being put into place, and because the root of the problem was not uncovered, whilst it may correct the issue in the short term and get them to conform, long-term the problem will just become worse.

The repercussion of this scenario is educational trauma. This is regardless of whether the child continues to stay in school or whether they end up leaving/being excluded. Examples of contributing factors for educational trauma could include negative interactions with the school, the feeling of being unsafe, discrimination, bullying, ineffective teaching, chronic stresses, focus on standardised testing when they cannot cope with this, or even special educational needs and disability needs that are unmet by the school.

CASE STUDY

I knew a child once who I met/taught in a therapeutic school. He had been excluded from mainstream school for issues relating to anger management and behavioural issues. Amongst some of the things I learnt about him as I got to know him over the years was that he didn't like the lighting in his old classroom. It triggered a sensory overload in him because the lights flickered ever so slightly. They were the old strip lights. Most of us would not notice this in a room but it completely distracted this child from his lessons each day and triggered heightened anxiety. This led to outbursts and other behavioural issues. Nobody at his previous school had ever picked this up. He was later permanently excluded. Was this a naughty child? Was there a different way this might have been dealt with more effectively?

How do you know if your child is suffering from educational trauma? What are the tell-tale signs? It can manifest itself in different ways and can look different from one child to another depending on what happened and how the child intrinsically deals with it. Resilience factors affect how bad the trauma can be.

Anxiety, avoidance, anger, depression, low self-esteem, decreased motivation, frustration, withdrawal and mental health issues are all typical symptoms of educational trauma. Until the trauma has been dealt with, the child will not feel safe enough to engage with learning – safety, love and nurturing have to come first. That part of the child's brain will not be ready to learn with formal learning, and trauma can potentially last a lifetime, so it is vital to be aware and address the matter if you see the signs.

Let's spare a thought for the parents in this situation. They have probably also fought for years for their child to be diagnosed, better understood or given the support they need to progress. Parents of SEND children usually know unquestionably that their child is not misbehaving or acting up. They know what their child actually needs is to be supported in a slightly different way than a neurotypical child. The school (and other professional organisations) have most likely had numerous conversations with the parent to let them know that their child is failing, misbehaving or not coping. This process can go on for years and can feel like a battle, which brings further stress into the home environment when the child is not at school.

There may be logistical issues or financial constraints already on the family, meaning that parents cannot just remove the child from school as they have to go to work or have a home life which makes it difficult for any kind of alternative to even be a consideration.

In situations where home education becomes the only choice, parents who are left to home educate their child or wait for an alternative provision to become available may have to give up their job and rethink what their day-to-day life would look like. For the most part, there is little funding for families who "choose" to home-educate. Those who require education, care and a healthcare plan (EHCP) for a SEND child may be entitled to some support (known as EOTAS), but the diagnosis, EHCP, and then the fight to get EOTAS funding is long and substantial. It can take years and be the source of its own trauma for both the parent and the child.

It is worth noting that this is also the biggest shift in home education over the last few years. Yes, there are still home educators who choose to home educate because of personal reasons such as travel, religion or the desire to educate their child in a particular way, but this is no longer the main motive for education in today's climate. We have online communities collectively consisting of around 20,000 families, almost all of whom are home-educating. We estimate that around 80% of these are home educating (and this was not their first choice. they wanted their child to access school).

Financial and emotional pressures are now added to a long list of the prospective day-to-day struggles they already have to face with having an SEN child. It can be a dark and painful journey for the entire family, which leads to feelings of inadequacy, confusion and a lack of direction.

According to ITV News in April 2024, it is estimated that the number of school exclusions is at its highest in the last twenty years. Approximately 22,000 children aged six or below were excluded or suspended from primary schools in England in 2022. 97% of these were SEN children. Simply putting the children back into the system again after a week away from school is not going to fix it either. It will create a new circle for the same events to repeat over and over again.

> *"If you keep judging a fish by its ability to climb a tree, it will spend its whole life thinking it is stupid."*
>
> — **Albert Einstein**

WHAT CAN YOU DO?

There is no one answer here. Every circumstance is different. If you are the child's primary caregiver or an educational professional working with the child, try to take a holistic, child-centred approach, rather than looking at what a main-stream, school-based system would want you to do. This is not a textbook question, so it requires more than just a text-book answer but here are some ways you can help children with education trauma:

BELIEVE AND VALIDATE THEIR FEELINGS

Regardless of whether you are the parent or an educational professional working with the child, it is important that you actively listen to them if they try to talk to you. Very often, children can be dismissed or their complaints not taken seriously enough. Let them know that they have been heard and that it is okay for them to not feel okay. Leave yourself or another support mechanism open for them in case they would like to talk again at a future date.

GATHER INFORMATION

Talk to the people who work with the child and try to gain an understanding of the bigger picture. Try and step into a day in the life of the child and pinpoint what is happening, when and with whom. Consider how severe the situation is and what resources might be available at the school to support them (if any). Share your findings with the school and work with them to see if you can find a route forward for the child. This route needs to offer the child an opportunity to deal with the trauma as well as access learning again – they will not be able to access learning by simply being present in a classroom if they are still feeling withdrawn, fearful, anxious or depressed.

SUPPORT THEIR NEEDS

School-based trauma can manifest itself in different ways so will need different types of support. In some instances, this may mean that you need to remove them from the situation in which they find themselves. In other instances, it may mean helping them find coping strategies, access to a therapist or just being patient and giving them some time with relaxation techniques or other creative outlets.

Assuming the child has been taken out of the mainstream school environment and either home-educated or educated in a different space, the next stage is to support that child to re-engage. Part of that support will include taking a break from a full learning timetable and re-evaluating where the child is. Remember, they need to feel safe and secure in their environment and to deal with whatever has happened before any active learning can take place. This is imperative to successful re-engagement.

During this period, the child may engage in therapy, take a break from all learning, or just need time to "play" (regardless of age). It is a good time to put in things like self-care, strategies to support positive mental health, offer time to talk with a trusted adult and focus very much on the child's well-being.

There is no length of time that this "should" take. When they are ready, they will start to show interest in wanting to do more/find out more about things. Again, this would not necessarily look like structured learning. If they came out of mainstream education because a linear approach to a curriculum did not work for them, there is a good chance that a linear approach to a curriculum will not work for them in an alternative environment either. A different approach is needed to get them to learn. This does not mean that they will not be able to engage in professional qualifications down the line. It just means that they need a different route to get there.

HEALING FROM TRAUMA

The good news is that there is a light at the end of this tunnel. If a child has been through trauma, there are strategies that will support their recovery from this, and putting these in place now is a helpful way to address the trauma and build in things that will give them resilience strategies that can last a lifetime.

All they need now is a helping hand to believe in themselves again and some self-confidence. It is not a time to do any kind of formal learning. Attempts to do so may result in things like refusal, meltdowns and further negative interactions. It is best to hang on for a while. Don't worry that they will fall behind or miss learning time. Learning cannot be forced; the child has to be in the right frame of mind to want to explore the world around them again. They will catch up when they are ready.

Start at the root. Understand what the reason was for the trauma in the first place. Why did it happen? Was it a prolonged period of time or a single incident that caused the trauma? Have any attempts been made to resolve any open issues?

Try to identify how the child is presenting. Is it anxiety? Reluctance? Depression? If it is anger, where does the anger come from? Usually, anger is an emotion that hides other emotions like fear. Address the issue. Have open conversations about it if you feel it is appropriate to do so. Here are some other ideas that can help to deal with trauma and get the child ready to move on and ready to learn again:

Safe spaces: Build dens and have corners where they can go and just exist if they wish to. Little areas in the garden, tents or even a cardboard box can be transformational for them. Involve them in decisions about safe spaces and give them plenty of options of places they can go if they feel as though they need a little bit of time out or want to be by themselves. They should be free to use those spaces as often as they like, whenever they feel as though they want to go there.

Emotional regulation: Practice things like grounding, breathing exercises, mindfulness, yoga, meditation, exercise or just about anything else you think they will engage in that will be good for their emotional regulation and well-being. You don't have to do all these things. Just pick one or two that work and do them regularly.

Consistency: Whatever the child's day or week looks like, you should try and keep some sort of consistency. Change is okay but try to limit this for a little while. The familiarity of knowing what is coming allows for a feeling of safety and helps to ease anxiety.

Involvement in decision-making: The more involved a young person feels in decisions that are about them, regardless of whether this is educational, mental-health related, or even just what their next meal is going to be, the more likely you are to get success from them in any particular situation. Even if it is a decision that you have to make on their behalf, try and give them an element of choice. For example, "We have to go to the doctor today. Do you want to walk, or go in the car?"

Choice of participation: If possible, let them say no from time to time. If they don't want to engage in something, try to give them an alternative option rather than just being a straightforward yes or no. For example, if you want them to engage with formal learning, like writing a story, but they do not want to do any writing that day, offer them the option to audio record it or to role-play something with their soft toys instead. If they don't want to do any of this, then offer them some mindfulness activities for that day instead. Repeat this as often as necessary. They will eventually engage when they are ready.

Visual schedules: Timetables, routine charts and just about anything that helps them to know what is coming and helps them to organise themselves day-to-day are really powerful tools. It takes away a lot of anxiety and they can be involved in putting it together as well. Taking control of their learning a little bit, and making some decisions for it, will mean that they enjoy it more.

WHAT MIGHT HOME EDUCATION LOOK LIKE?

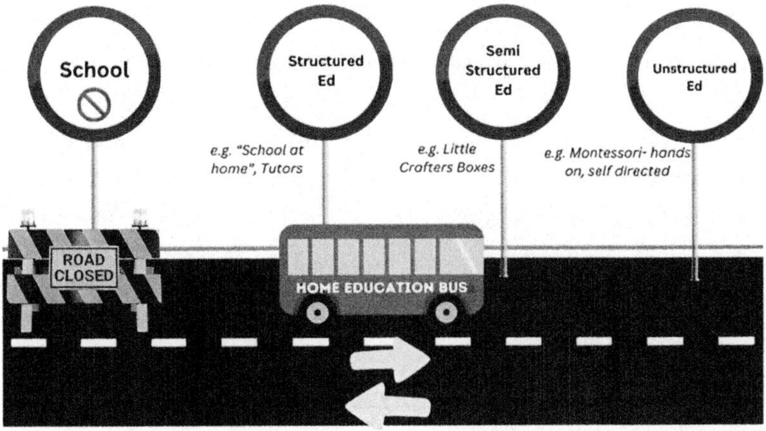

Home educating can vary hugely. There are no rules or any one correct way in which it should go. Family wishes, child needs and available resources all play a part in the decision-making process and that is before one starts to consider which philosophies will work well.

There is, however, some common ground that many home-educating communities share. It is a bit like a bus route on a road map. It starts at school, where things either did not work out or the family elected not to send the child in the first place. Many will start with a more structured approach of what they think home education should look like – a "school at home" style environment, which may be made up of structured formal learning time, tutors and set times when the child is expected to engage with education. This is more of a teacher-centred approach, even if the parent is acting as the teacher in that situation.

Some people stay with this model or maintain some form of teacher-led learning, but many find this labour-intensive and observe reluctance in the child because of the environment they created. "School", in its most traditional sense, did not work for the child in the first place. Creating the same environment at home is starting down the same path where they have already failed before. The adult, without realising it, has also been raised in a world where structure and behaviourism are all they know, so they don't realise that they don't have to do it this way.

Then might come the next stop: Unstructured Education. Many home-educating families often use the term "unlearning" or "unschooling" to describe the process of continuing a less structured approach at home. In its extreme, this is the opposite of the first stop. Completely self-directed and child-led, it is entirely left to the child to decide everything from the time of day learning takes place to the environment and topic of learning. The adult acts as a facilitator of the learning rather than a teacher. They only teach something if the child asks them to. This approach relies on the thought process that children are predisposed to learn and will learn through playing and interacting with the environment around them.

Natural curiosity is very powerful in a learning environment. It creates an attitude shift in the learner from feeling like they have to follow a particular pattern of learning to naturally wanting to seek out the answers themselves. A curiosity-led (or interest-led) approach can be a game changer, particularly for learners who may otherwise struggle to access traditional learning. Passion fuels motivation and creates a positive learning environment, regardless of age. If the educator can find a way to tap into this curiosity or passion of the learner, they will have their undivided attention!

Some families try this approach and continue with this because it works so well with the child. Others find themselves struggling because it is too unstructured for them. They want some freedom, but with some structure, too. They continue on their journey and at some point, they find a new stop. This is somewhere between structured and semi-structured. It could be something like having formal learning for a couple of hours in the morning with a tutor, then progressing on to more child-led learning in the afternoon. Alternatively, it could be something like the Little Crafters Boxes progressive learning approach, where they choose what structural units of work they wish to achieve each month (in a project-led approach) out of an extensive list and complete just those that interest them.

A semi-structured approach is where the majority of home-educating families find their happy place. This is also a wonderful compromise between getting interest-led, autonomous learning, yet still maintaining some structure in a world where this is still going to be an important factor for them as they grow up.

OTHER FACTORS TO CONSIDER

There are other important factors, too, which create a purposeful and optimal learning environment. For instance, trust and safety play vital roles. The child can only tap into the part of their brain where they are able to learn once these other human needs are met. For some children, this is where it breaks down for them in schools. The loss of trust or safety leads to behavioural shifts or anxieties which, in turn, end in negative experiences which can take the form of isolation, exclusion or other school-based trauma.

For those children, it is important to rebuild that trust or safety net before any education provision can be effective. This step, in itself, is a therapeutic measure. No amount of time should be put on it either – listening to the child involved and working at their pace is fundamental to the success of this phase. They will move on to learning when they feel ready and engaged themselves. Children's minds are naturally curious once they are in the right frame of mind to take in new things from the world around them. Nobody can learn in "fight or flight" mode.

Parents often need time to heal too. they may have been in a situation where they have been battling the system, waiting for months for a diagnosis or waiting for support to commence. This process can take years and feel never-ending or impossible to navigate. To have this on top of the additional job of supporting an SEN child can push many families to breaking point. It is therefore important for the whole family to take some time to heal, consider the approach that they will next adopt for education and focus on methods that build trust and cater to the individual needs of the child and those of the wider family.

If home education is the next step, creating a safe learning space, incorporating play-based learning or employing individual learning plans are good places to start. Alternatively, a smaller school or provision that can meet the needs of the child may be a good option. If this (vital) phase is implemented effectively and with some thought, it can be transformative for the child and life-changing for the entire family. This, after all, is a new beginning and an opportunity for the child to regain confidence, find joy in learning and acquire new strategies to support themselves and their needs – something they may never have learnt to do until this point.

Once a therapeutic, meaningful learning environment has been established, it is time to ponder the "How" of your learning provision. Regardless of whether it is an alternative provision or home education, the question is the same – "What am I going to teach?". Do you resort to following the national curriculum or something similar to this? Perhaps a topic of choice will help create some curiosity and re-engage the child. Or perhaps this is not the time to be thinking about structured learning. The options can be mind-boggling and we will look at different teaching philosophies in the next chapter, but a good way to start is to look at where the child is at and consider what they need right now.

WHEN IS THE RIGHT TIME TO START?

No matter how beautiful or meaningful a learning space is, nobody will learn in it until they are mentally ready or "in that space" metaphorically speaking. They need to feel safe and secure in their environment before their brain is even ready to engage with any new learning.

Give the child time to deal with any trauma they may have encountered and to get accustomed to their new learning environment. You will know they are ready when they start asking questions about things and showing natural curiosity about the world around them. It varies from one child to another, but anything from "What is for lunch today?" to "Why is the sky blue?" are all indicators that they are now feeling ready to learn again.

This is where Maslow's hierarchy of needs comes in. Foundational needs like safety and security must be met before the child can focus on learning and higher-order (critical thinking) learning needs like self-actualisation.

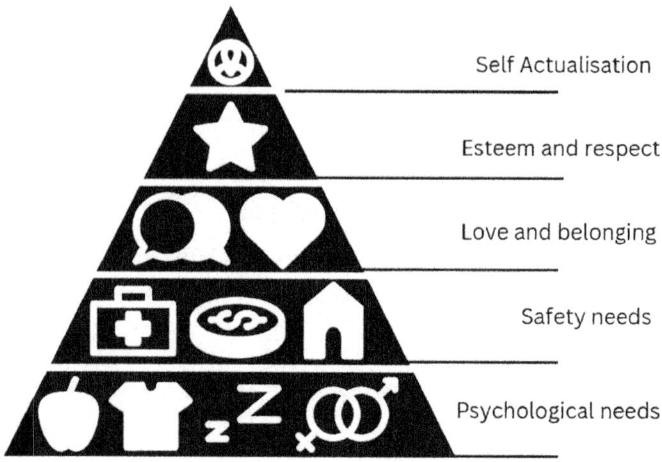

In a nutshell, this model suggests that human needs must be met (in order) from the bottom up. You can't jump up a level without having all the needs on the below levels met. Also, if there is a life-changing event, trauma or something that rattles something from one of the lower levels, you have to go back to that stage and ensure everything is intact before resuming at the upper levels. Note that self-actualisation (higher-order thinking and learning) is right at the top. If you are worried that the child will miss learning time or need to engage in learning, regardless of where they are at, this model suggests otherwise. They cannot learn until all these other needs are met.

Evidence that the child is transitioning into a more "ready to learn" state presents itself when they start to do things like become curious about the world around them, start to engage in social conversations, smile more or seem visibly more relaxed.

It is important not to worry. The child will engage with learning when they are ready. Humans are all naturally curious. As soon as they feel more settled, they will start to ask questions and engage. This may be small snippets to start with but it is a starting point.

They are not going to fall behind or need to catch up. We all learn and acquire knowledge at different speeds and using different strategies. Furthermore, children especially have the most amazing ability to "catch up" with missed learning when they are in the right frame of mind and they actually want to do it.

School-based trauma, low self-esteem, additional learning needs and negative experiences of/ attitudes to education are all obstacles that may well need to be moved or made manageable once the decision to home-educate or use an alternative provision has been made.

Either way, establish positive relationships, build trust and be guided by the pace of the child. Nobody can learn while in "fight or flight" mode. No amount of time should be placed on this phase either. After all, there is learning happening in this phase too, such as social and emotional skills, trust building, communication, etc. Just because these are not academic qualifications, this does not make them any less important.

When the child is starting to be ready, an interest-based approach is a really good place to start. Indulge the questions that they are asking- respond to the curiosity with further questions, e.g. " I'm not sure, shall we investigate this together?" and create "rabbit holes" for them to fall into if they wish to. It is still a good time to not worry about formal learning or national curriculum. Instead, play, be curious together and give them opportunities to explore the world around them. This will provide a lovely transition back into learning and feel very different to what they had once experienced with a behaviour approach.

In many cases, the change is so subtle that they don't even realise that they are learning.

CHAPTER FOUR

UNLEASHING POTENTIAL – IS THERE A "BEST" WAY TO LEARN?

Is there a "best" way to learn or some magic strategy that we should all be using?

The short answer is "No". If there were, everyone who wants to be an educator would be taken to one side and shown the correct way.

The truth is, there are a plethora of ways to do it and no one way is better than another. Every philosophy that underpins learning has its pros and cons and should be considered with equal weight alongside the needs of the child, the wider family and the environment/resources available.

Later in the chapter, we delve into some of the philosophies that can be used when you are ready to approach learning again, but first, let's look at the benefits the flexibility of considering different philosophies can offer. Just having knowledge that the different philosophies exist will help you to be more confident and open-minded in planning your next steps.

FINDING THE SWEET SPOT

The circadian rhythm is the body's natural clock. We all have our unique body clocks, which are better at focusing at certain times of the day than others. We all have different amounts that we like to sleep and some of us even refer to ourselves as "night owls" or "early birds".

Mainstream schooling needs a more regimented approach, where children have to attend at a certain time of day for a particular number of days in the year. This is the same every day, and there is no flexibility around this approach. This is because they have thousands of learners to push through the system and there is less flexibility to allow for the logistics of anything different. Most children will find a way to make this work and train their bodies to be able to access this.

Neurodivergent learners sometimes struggle with this approach. This could be because they have autism and struggle to sleep at night. It could be pathological demand avoidance that prevents them from being able to follow a rigid routine. It might be a short attention span or a physical disability that makes it difficult for a child to sit for prolonged periods and learn. The variations are infinite. The point is that one size does not fit all.

An alternative education approach sometimes is able to provide more flexibility. It could mean that there is an opportunity to observe the child with the mindset of still being aligned with their wishes, and their circadian rhythms. This will help them to access learning and provide a clear path, whereby they are being set up to succeed. But what would this look like? It could be a small change like letting them work in the evening when they struggle to sleep, or encouraging them to lie on the floor in a comfortable outfit while they listen to important information (rather than sitting on a chair at a desk).

The content itself does not have to be confined to the national curriculum either. It often works well to not follow such a traditional approach initially, even if only for a short time. Learning is most effective when there is a balance between interest and challenge. Going "too deep" and trying to re-engage them with a curriculum that led to the initial trauma, could have an adverse effect at this foundational stage.

These small tweaks could be the difference that they needed all along and the difference between success and failure.

We are now beginning to look at the whole child. We are beginning to consider all their needs, not just their educational ones. They have a place where they feel safe, are finding coping strategies for their triggers and the adults working with them are trusted to meet their needs (or at least try hard to). Whatever content is taught has a far higher chance of success now because we are meeting the other needs of the child at the same time and starting from where they are rather than where we expect them to be.

Positive emotions like curiosity and engagement enhance learning, while negative emotions like fear and anxiety can hinder it. Angry children having meltdowns or sad children in despair are not going to learn, no matter how much one tries to force the issue. Putting them in a chair in a classroom against their will or isolating them with a textbook will have no positive effect on moving them forward. It may tick an attendance box or a progress sheet for a teacher who needs to show that the student has had the opportunity to access the content, but no actual learning will happen if the emotional state of the child is not in a good place. Therapeutic educators can help foster positive emotions by creating a supportive atmosphere, using humour and celebrating successes.

The same applies to us all. If we consider our own learning needs, regardless of what we are learning and how we best acquire knowledge, the process is not something that can be forced upon us at any time that is appropriate for the educator. Environment, emotions and state of mind are all important factors to how successful or effective this can be at any given time.

DIFFERENT APPROACHES TO LEARNING

There are a plethora of philosophies to learning which underpin the different approaches. In the UK, behaviourist philosophy underpins not only a huge part of the education system but also that of many workplaces. The use of repeating desired behaviours for rewards and sanctioning less desirable behaviours is key in this practice. The approach works well for conditioning and maintaining a level of control in structured learning. However, it is less effective for critical thinking and interest/passion-led learning or working.

All the different philosophies have their advantages and disadvantages and for those children who fall out of the mainstream education system, it is often the case that a different approach is necessary.

Let's take a deeper dive into some of the main philosophies.

TEACHER-CENTRED LEARNING

Teacher-centred philosophies are those where there is an educator who is in charge of planning and delivering the learning content. Traditionally, the child will absorb the information given and then do something with that information to show that they have learned it. Let's look at some teacher-centred approaches.

ESSENTIALISM

This is when basic skills such as reading, writing, arithmetic and conduct are taught by the adult to help children master core knowledge. It is a sort of "back to basics" approach. It is about prioritising our thoughts to be the most important tasks and focusing energy and resources on teaching one thing, or a small group of things, that are thought to be the most important.

An example of this could be that a family decides that all the GCSEs are not important, and the child has shown an interest in geography, so they focus all their effort on supporting the child to gain lots of knowledge in geography, with the other basic skills that they might need to find employment within that field.

Another example could be that if a family-run business, such as agricultural farming, has children within it who do not access the schooling system, the child might instead be brought up on a farm, learning the essential skills needed to take over the farming business once they are old enough. Just the essential skills are taught, with little emphasis on qualifications or anything that is not needed for the child's future in the business.

The advantages of this strategy are that the child gains in-depth knowledge in something that they have an interest in from a young age. The disadvantages of the strategy are that they don't get an opportunity to explore things and may change their mind down the line, leaving a skills gap.

PERENNIALISM

This is another teacher-centred approach, with a structured classroom environment, where it is thought that by studying the works of great thinkers, students can develop a deep understanding of what they are taught and prepare themselves to be thoughtful, informed citizens.

Subjects like religious studies, history or geography may play a large part of perennialist teaching. Ideas are everlasting and lifted from great books of the past. Literature, philosophy, and history are very common to see in a perennialist approach.

This is commonly used in religious schools, for example, where a particular faith is taught in detail alongside only the core subjects. This approach is rarely used in solitude. It is often incorporated with some of the other philosophies such as progressivism or behaviourism.

The advantages of this philosophy are that it has strong foundations with a solid academic base, it provides timeless knowledge with a sense of historical perspective and cultural literacy and often emphasises moral and ethical values. The disadvantages of this approach are that its relevance is limited and can sometimes be out of date. Sometimes, there is a neglect of contemporary issues, for example, a religious school might not teach the theory of evolution in science because they don't want children to know that there is a choice in belief systems. It can also limit creativity and individual interests with its rigid curriculum.

BEHAVIOURISM

The behaviourist approach is what a traditional mainstream school currently looks like (for the most part). It is all about behaviour through observation and uses the idea of conditioning by rewarding good behaviour and sanctioning poor behaviour, with the thought process that eventually, only the desirable behaviour will emerge. The curriculum is fixed and progress is measured.

The advantages of this approach are that it allows for a teacher-centred approach, whereby lots of children can be taught at once and an element of control is retained by the teacher in the content and the overall behaviour. The disadvantages of this approach are that it does not allow for critical thinking or interest-led learning. Another disadvantage of this approach is that it has no scope for grey areas like undesirable behaviours that are uncontrollable or occur as a result of external factors which are not the fault of the child. The child always gets sanctioned, which is not always the correct way if the behaviour is out of their control.

One of the biggest disadvantages of the behaviourist system is that the internal thoughts, feelings and motivations are completely disregarded as they cannot be directly observed. It is almost entirely about extrinsic motivation and mental health needs are not regarded as important in the learning process.

STUDENT-CENTRED PHILOSOPHIES

PROGRESSIVISM

This philosophy believes that education comes from experience – learning through doing. It has a belief system in progress and changes being fundamental to human development. It focuses on the individual needs and interests of the child, emphasises hands-on learning, project work and real-world experiences, taking into consideration student's lives and the world around them (so progressive approaches can look different for different children). It also recognises and accommodates diverse learning and different learning styles.

An example of a progressivism approach is Little Crafters Boxes (with LCB Education). It uses a holistic, progressivism philosophy in part of its offering, project-based learning is fundamental and subjects are all connected holistically as part of a bigger enquiry and investigation opportunity.

Some of the advantages of this philosophy are that it engages student interests and fosters a love of learning and autonomy. It also encourages critical thinking skills, problem-solving skills and collaboration. The learning is relevant to students' lives in the real world.

The disadvantages are that it can be time-consuming to implement in mass and would require a significant change to the current curriculum system and assessment practices to bring this into mainstream schooling. It would mean a complete overhaul of the current system. It is also more difficult to measure or quantify (unlike a curriculum within a behaviourist approach) and leaves the potential for uneven learning outcomes if not implemented well.

CONSTRUCTIVISM

Constructivism uses the idea of children building on their own prior thoughts to construct their own understanding and knowledge base of a particular topic rather than passively receiving information in a teacher-centred philosophy. It takes an interest of a child and, through an inquiry-based route, builds it over time to advance the learning of a particular topic. Learning can be advanced through collaboration and interaction with others and children reflect on their experiences and adjust their understanding accordingly. It is a real-world learning approach.

in a nutshell, this is practical learning. For example, rather than giving a child a textbook on ecosystems, they may be asked to create their own ecosystem and observe it over time to see what it does. They are gaining knowledge first-hand, rather than passively learning it from a book or a teacher. The adult is just facilitating the learning in that scenario to help the child, to the learning and understanding part themselves.

This is another philosophy that is very much part of the offer of Little Crafters Boxes and LCB Education. Children are encouraged to learn practically, through crafts, experimentation and going out into the real world to investigate things themselves. As it is remote learning for the most part, the teachers within the company act as facilitators, providing them with everything they need to be able to jump into rabbit holes themselves and construct their own knowledge.

The obvious advantages of this style of learning are that it is interest-led and student-centred. It encourages deeper understanding and learning, promotes social interaction and collaboration, improves student motivation and engagement and increases knowledge retention.

The disadvantage is that it requires prior knowledge through a different philosophy to be viable – you need a thought that has already been planted to be able to build upon it. On a mass scale, this would be hard to implement within the current schooling system because it requires a shift in thinking from the teacher becoming the leader of the learning to becoming the facilitator of the learning. In some cases, children may need additional support in self-directed learning, so it can be challenging to do it completely remotely.

EXISTENTIALISM

Existentialism is an extreme version of self-directed learning, which is completely interest-led and directed by the child. It works upon the thought process that learning is predisposed and children will learn themselves through play and their environment. The adult is very much the facilitator and rarely directs any kind of learning. They wait for the child to approach them if they require support with whatever ideas they are working on at any given time.

Existentialism focuses very much on the child's unique learning journey and allows them to go at their own pace, with complete freedom of choice and the opportunity to truly be themselves and to pursue their passions.

This can be challenging to implement in a fully traditional educational setting because it requires a complete overhaul in thinking from teacher-centred learning. Behaviourists would argue that there is not enough control in this method and that learning cannot be easily observed or measured. The structure is more relaxed and this can sometimes create existential anxiety (a sense of too much choice). It requires highly skilled teachers with in-depth knowledge of the different philosophies to truly be able to implement the style of learning.

There are some huge advantages to existentialism when it is done well. It massively encourages critical thinking, creativity and innovation. It builds resilience by helping children cope with uncertainty and challenges and also inspires a lifelong love of learning because they have a sense of purpose and meaning in education.

WHICH PHILOSOPHY IS THE BEST?

There is no best one. All the philosophies have research to suggest they work to a point, and all of them have their pros and cons. The best philosophy is one that takes into consideration the needs and desires of the child and how they learn best.

A blended approach is usually better than using a single philosophy to an extreme, as it allows for a more rounded education overall.

CHAPTER FIVE

UNLEARNING THE LABELS – EMBRACING GROWTH OVER GRADES

Let's delve into a crucial aspect of therapeutic education: moving beyond labels and fostering a growth mindset in both educators and learners. We'll explore the pitfalls of labelling children based on achievement levels and explore strategies for promoting a love of learning that prioritises progress over perfection.

Every single time you hear a voice in your head that says that the child is behind, or not matching the progress of their peers or that they have missed learning, remind yourself that you are comparing them against observations in a behaviourist system. It was a system that didn't work for them, and that's why they are here. Let's stop comparing children to each other and trying to measure how much they have learned. Learning is not something that should be quantified. The only benefit of this is that schools can make sure they have met their targets and can compare their practice against other schools. There is very little benefit to the learner.

The objective of education should not be the amount of quantifiable progress a child can make, but more on how much they engage and love what they are learning about. If you were ever going to measure any kind of progress, therapeutically, you should measure the state of their mental health, strategies for self-care and the critical thinking that they demonstrate day-to-day. These things far outweigh whether they can recite every phonic they were ever taught, or how many GCSEs they will achieve.

PROGRESS

So, why do we use labels for children's progress in an educational setting? This is an age-old debate with lots of grey areas within the education system. There is pressure on schools for children to make certain levels of progress for the school to be deemed good or outstanding by OFSTED (the Office for Standards in Education in England). There are also league tables, whereby schools are compared to one another based on the amount of progress that children have made on paper. This, in itself, begs the question of whether the progress that the child has made is actual progress, or progress that has been manufactured as data to make the school look as good as possible.

Behaviourists would argue that progress can identify strengths and weaknesses, provide benchmarks and even boost confidence and encourage continued effort in students. There is also the belief system that measuring progress provides insights into a child's academic and social development and helps parents to make informed choices about the child's education, because if you can't quantify progress then it is hard to measure if the child has moved forward throughout a period of time, right? This belief is then added to by the suggestion that they should be at a certain level by a certain age in various areas, to make the correct amount of progress by the time they leave the education system. Ideally, they need to make exactly the right amount of progress at every stage of their education. Too much or too little provides challenges for teachers within the system. Having been a teacher in the system, I have seen children not be pushed further if they have met their targets for that year, because they are no longer deemed a priority in the overall targets for that teacher or the school. Conversely, I have seen less able children feel like they are failing if they are unable to keep up with their peers because the number on a piece of paper that quantifies their progress is very real to them.

With "more able" children, does this mean that they will never reach their true potential in areas where they are particularly interested and can do more than the average child in their class?

Although this is not always the case, of course, it happens. Class sizes are huge and the teacher has to prioritise those children who have not quite got there yet, or they will be reprimanded for not meeting targets. This leads to boredom and a lack of engagement in the top performers within that class. It also places a ceiling on the amount of progress that they can make at a given time. Furthermore, because the curriculum is set, the teachers themselves may not have the subject knowledge to push them further than the curriculum allows.

With "less able" children, do they ever truly fulfil their potential if they are labelled as less intelligent on paper than their peers? No matter how nicely we dress this up in a school report, failure still feels like failure to them.

The other side of the argument is that progress should not be quantified or measured. Children should be met at whatever level they are at, and no amount of progress is too little or too much. Only when one removes the barriers and the pressure of learning, does it allow for more effective and enjoyable learning to take place in an environment where the child is not feeling judged.

Let's compare this to an example of an adult working in an office. How would that adult feel if the employer walked around with a clipboard all day, assessing the efficiency of the worker, and ran periodical tests to see if typing speed had improved or telephone manners had become more efficient? What if the employer took it one step further and wrote an annual report for that worker with a red, amber and green system to suggest how they had gotten on throughout the year in comparison to all the other workers in the office? Would this be an effective way to run one's workforce? No, it would not be. So why do we expect children to perform at their best when we treat them in a similar fashion?

Labels are useful for the educator and for the bigger system but can be counterproductive for the child. This is even more so for those children who are not at the "top of the class" and are struggling to meet the targets that are put upon them. It can have a massive effect on a child's self-esteem if they are constantly "underperforming" according to their labels and in comparison with their peers. This message can stay with them for the rest of their lives.

Why is this widely accepted and not talked about more? Because we, the adults, are products of the same system. Many don't even realise there might be a different way. Then there is the big institution syndrome to contend with. This is because it is a system that has been going for years and provided by the government (in essence, an organisation that we are continually persuaded to trust), so it feels absurd for anyone to question it.

Can you think of any feelings that manifested themselves like this when you were at school and are still with you now? Is this what we truly want for our children? When people say, "I went through it and it never did me any harm", what does this "harm" look like? Merely that they survived or got a job after leaving? The truth is that If there is insecurity, fear of failure, lack of motivation or even bullying incidents, these moments and scars will stay with you for the rest of your life. Is this not harmful?

Of course, we can't expect a perfect system that protects us from everything – after all, life happens, and we are bound to have both positive and negative experiences throughout that time. However, statistics show there is an increasing number of children who are falling through the system now because it has failed them so badly. There are more than 100,000 children in the UK currently sitting at home, waiting for alternative provisions to become available for them. They are currently not receiving any kind of proper education.

Labels can be dangerous, limiting a child's potential and impacting their confidence. This can lead to learned helplessness and fear of failure. A growth mindset, however, and the power of "yet" can be a game changer. This approach emphasises the journey of learning and celebrates effort over innate ability.

TOOLS TO SUPPORT PROGRESS

MINDSET

Stanford psychologist, Carol Dweck, identified two primary mindsets that shape our outlook on learning: growth mindset and fixed mindset. Those with a **fixed mindset** believe intelligence and talent are fixed traits. They see challenges as a threat, fearing failure will expose a lack of inherent ability. Conversely, a **growth mindset** views intelligence and talent as malleable. It emphasises the power of effort and dedication in developing our skills and knowledge. Challenges become opportunities for growth and setbacks are stepping stones on the path to mastery.

The simple word "yet" packs a powerful punch when it comes to fostering a growth mindset. When we say, "I can't do this," we reinforce a fixed mindset. However, by adding "yet", we acknowledge the current state while opening the door to future possibilities. "I can't solve this problem yet" becomes a springboard for action. It empowers us to seek help, persevere through difficulty and ultimately achieve success.

A growth mindset fosters a lifelong love of learning. It allows the child to embrace challenges with curiosity and a willingness to learn. Benefits include:

- **Resilience:** The learner bounces back from setbacks with a "not yet" attitude and stays motivated in the face of difficulty.
- **Effort and Dedication:** The learner understands that success requires hard work and persistence, leading to a greater sense of accomplishment.
- **Embrace of Challenges:** The learner sees challenges as opportunities to learn and grow, rather than roadblocks to our goals.
- **Lifelong Learning:** The learner develops a passion for learning that extends beyond the classroom and enriches their entire lives.

This tool is one that we can all use more, regardless of what philosophy, approach or even institution we find ourselves in. A growth mindset can be incredibly powerful in all areas of life.

PRAISE

Personalised praise is a really powerful tool. Authentic praise, that is saying something like "I love how you used a diagram to solve that problem!" instead of the generic praise "You're so smart!", is more impactful and meaningful.

We must praise effort just as much as we praise achievement. The journey is as important as the destination itself. It helps with intrinsic motivation and praise can be used to help them have a more growth-oriented mindset. For example, to say something like "I loved that you found that challenging but you tried again and again until you got it" or "It was really nice to see you asking questions because you were curious about this bit", can be so encouraging.

Using praise in this way makes the learner more reflective on the journey that they had to get to the solution or the end of the task. It makes them think about the way in which they learned and then the strategies that they used.

If a child has a negative experience during the task that was set, for example, let's say they had a meltdown or could not complete the work that was given to them, still try and find a positive in what they did do (for example, that they tried, or put lots of effort into the bit that they did do). Also, try to return to the task at a later date and adopt a different strategy to try and complete all or part of it. This will provide lots of scope to add some praise about perseverance and turning a failure into a triumph.

These strategies – authentic praise and not labelling the child or having expectations of their progress – all focus on the intrinsic value of learning and personal growth, rather than extrinsic rewards like grades. It is therapeutic and holistically focused.

As soon as the child does not feel like they are being judged, they will start to be more curious, enjoy learning more and become more independent in their approach. Our brains are naturally curious. If a child has stopped accessing that part of the brain for whatever reason, remember that it means you have to go back some steps and work on the safety/nurture element with them again until they are ready. There is no need to force the issue. When they are ready, they will just learn!

The effectiveness of praise relies on understanding how we learn and how different approaches view the role of praise.

A simple "well done" might seem harmless, but the science behind praise reveals a fascinating interplay between motivation, mindset, and knowledge acquisition. Let's look at praise from different approaches to learning.

Constructivism emphasises the importance of student agency in constructing knowledge. Here, praise that focuses on the process of learning can be particularly effective.

Praising a student for their perseverance when tackling a difficult problem, or their creativity in approaching a task, acknowledges their effort and fosters a growth mindset. Dweck's work on growth mindset highlights the importance of praising effort and strategies over simply praising intelligence. A student who believes their intelligence is fixed might be discouraged by setbacks, whereas a student with a growth mindset sees challenges as opportunities to learn and improve.

Behaviourism, with its focus on observable behaviours, utilises praise as a form of positive reinforcement. When a student exhibits a desired behaviour, like completing their homework or participating in class discussions, praise acts as a reward, strengthening the likelihood of that behaviour being repeated. However, behaviourists often emphasise the importance of varying rewards and tailoring praise to the individual student. Over-reliance on generic praise can diminish its effectiveness.

Ultimately, the most impactful praise is specific, sincere and focused on the learning process itself. By understanding the different approaches to learning, educators can craft praise that motivates, reinforces positive behaviours and fosters a love of learning that extends far beyond the classroom walls.

Regardless of philosophy, an overall **therapeutic** approach prioritises a student's emotional well-being and self-esteem. Here, praise becomes a tool for building confidence and fostering a positive relationship with learning.

- **Effort and progress take centre stage:** Therapeutic praise acknowledges the hard work and dedication a student puts into learning, not just the outcome. This can be particularly valuable for students who face academic challenges. Highlighting their effort and progress, even in small steps, reinforces their sense of self-efficacy and motivates them to keep trying.
- **Building self-esteem:** Unconditional positive regard is a cornerstone of therapy. Similarly, therapeutic praise avoids comparisons or academic judgements. Instead, it focuses on the student's unique strengths and celebrates their individual achievements. This helps build a strong sense of self-worth and fosters a belief in their ability to learn and grow.
- **Intrinsic motivation is key:** While other approaches might use praise as a form of reinforcement, the therapeutic approach aims to cultivate intrinsic motivation. By acknowledging a student's effort and celebrating their progress, praise fosters a sense of internal satisfaction and joy in learning, independent of external rewards.

REAL-WORLD APPROACHES TO HOME EDUCATION

A therapeutic learning approach can be adopted with any of the education philosophies. Here are some examples of how home education may be delivered. Each of these is therapeutic in its own way because learning has been tailored to focus on the individual needs of each of the children in the scenario.

CASE STUDY ONE

> *"We are mainly child-led with slight guidance, crossed with unschooling.*
>
> *We trust Woody to forge his own path of learning, which can be difficult when the wobbles set in, but just this week Woody, his dad and I have been doing quizzes online. We made flags of the world and Woody won. We did countries around the globe and Woody won. We have not studied the flags of the world or where on the globe countries are, yet he knew more than us. The knowledge of flags and countries has come from Woody playing FIFA and spending time on a device following his interest in football.*
>
> *We also did general knowledge quizzes and we were astounded at how much general knowledge Woody had. We put his general knowledge down to him living the home education life. He isn't at school, learning a specific curriculum; he is at home learning anything and everything.*
>
> *Home education really works for us because we trust the process of Woody learning his way."*
>
> — **Ruth Bibby**

CASE STUDY TWO

"We use a sort of a holistic, experimental, guided, interest-based approach – a mix of styles depending on topic, mood and capacity to cope.

He has this wonderful ability to make things, a keen eye for detail and a desire to learn at a deeper level. His artistic skills and interests in nature and history are a joy to see.

He has gone from being written off academically to thriving. From burnout/survival mode to happy, confident and valued."

— Lisa Davies

CASE STUDY THREE

"Phinley, thirteen, and Ezra, five, are both visual and kinaesthetic learners. We use the visual to learn and then kinaesthetics to embed. However, they also learn via audio when it is self-directed, often via YouTube videos, just listening whilst they're playing or building Lego.

They're very sensory, so need sensory input at the same time. So, we do lots of practical learning such as forest school, science experiments, cookery classes, equine therapy, snow sports, archery, fencing and swimming. We focus on sensory input to reduce anxiety and stimulate focus, but based on what they enjoy.

Everything is about what they enjoy. We had practical first aid sessions, exotic animal visits and visits to museums for photography and illusions etc. For an upcoming shark topic, they will be diving with them to embed it.

For an upcoming mythical creatures topic, the horse centre said they could transform one of their horses into a unicorn. These sorts of activities really help. There is a lot of play-focused learning, too.

Any written work is dictated orally for me to transcribe. There are lots of learning styles. I know our boys are mainly kinaesthetic but we tailor the other ways of learning to their needs and interests and they don't even notice."

— **Gayle Parker**

CASE STUDY FOUR

"Leon is, without doubt, a visual, hands-on learner, which expands his mind to be inquisitive. If he has a window with a good outside view, you can hear the cogs of his brain ticking over. Leon can be a reluctant learner, especially when his learning topic mainly involves pen-and-paper work, so we often have mindfulness days which we call "No Pen Friday".

We have done things like close our eyes whilst listening to pieces of music, identifying how the music makes us feel, sitting in the garden at night-time listening to nocturnal nature and had lots and lots of questions on space which has often resulted in debates. We incorporate lots of rest and relaxation to reset and speak of any anxieties, what Leon has enjoyed the past week and what he would like to learn more about."

— **Sarah Magowan**

CASE STUDY FIVE

"Ben is eleven and Alex is thirteen. They both have different learning styles.

Alex will tell you himself he is a visual learner. He absorbs information from videos and infographics so quickly. He also likes audio learning and absorbs audiobooks like a sponge. He thinks in pictures and loves visuals to support everything. He is very lively and movement-based. His "still" is everyone else's frantic fidgeting. He cannot sit and read a book for love nor money. He finds it difficult to absorb anything he reads and writing is a nightmare for him. He likes to speak his answers so he can pace around. To help at home, we write on windows and whiteboards while standing (and moving). We utilise online video websites and I make him books to support the learning. We never sit at a desk; we jump feet first into rabbit holes and we do a lot of hands-on learning with LCB. We use a Kindle Scribe, if writing is needed, and education programmes. He often texts me the answers to his learning, too.

Ben is a different kettle of fish. He happily sits at a desk so long as he can get up and wander around. He likes to have his kittens with him to help regulate and uses a wobble stool a lot. He gets up and down a lot, but we just roll with that. We put a sensory rug in the room we learn in and he loves lying on that and stroking it and we do a lot of out and about learning. He likes to go places and see things or be out in the garden or nature. He likes to use Lego, make models and experiment. He has an electronic device for recording answers but will use pen and paper too. The more creative the activity, the more he learns."

— Laura Bird

CHAPTER SIX

IGNITING CURIOSITY

Interest-led learning, historically, is always going to be a better way to engage, or re-engage, a child back into learning than formal, sit-down, curriculum-based learning. Why is this, though? For the most part, it is because interest-led learning creates intrinsic motivation. In other words, there is something inside us that is curious and wants to know more about certain things and is willing to invest time and effort into learning. Behaviourism does not allow for this because it is not something that can be observed, but there is plenty of research to suggest that it exists and that it is far more powerful than extrinsic motivation (physical rewards). In this chapter, we will dive into what intrinsic and extrinsic motivation look like and how they can drive the will to learn.

INTRINSIC MOTIVATION

The intrinsic value of learning refers to the enjoyment, satisfaction and personal growth gained from the learning process itself, independent of external rewards or pressures. It's about the inherent joy of discovery, the thrill of understanding a new concept, and the sense of accomplishment that comes with mastering a skill.

Here's a breakdown of the intrinsic value of learning:

Motivation: Children who experience the intrinsic value of learning are naturally curious and motivated to explore new ideas and challenges. They approach learning with a sense of excitement and a desire to understand the world around them.

Deeper Understanding: When learning is driven by intrinsic motivation, students are more likely to delve deeper into subjects and develop a richer understanding. They're not just memorising facts for a test, but actively seeking connections and building a strong knowledge base.

Lifelong Learning: The intrinsic value of learning fosters a love of learning that extends far beyond the classroom. Students who enjoy the process of learning are more likely to become lifelong learners, continuing to explore and grow throughout their lives.

Daniel Pink, author of "Drive", believes that the things that truly drive us are:

1. **Autonomy** – the desire for control over our work, the freedom to make our own decisions and the ability to feel like we own our projects. For example, in a therapeutic learning environment, this could be an opportunity for the learner to be given some control of their own learning, i.e., the learning topic (if this is possible), the strategy that is used (e.g., written activity or a visit somewhere), the learning environment or even the time of day that the learning activity will take place (this may be "Option A" or "Option B" rather than complete open choice depending on the time constraints available).
2. **Mastery** – the drive to get better at what we do, to learn and grow and to feel a sense of accomplishment from mastering a skill. Everyone likes to feel like they are the expert in something. There is a huge sense of accomplishment in feeling as though one has learned, understood and made some progress in the topic with which they are engaging. Think about learning a new language in another country. It can be incredibly frustrating at the beginning You may not understand the language, but then, through exposure to the language, you pick up a few simple words ("bonjour!").

There is a huge intrinsic motivation factor in making progress and turning those words into sentences or learning different topics to speak about.

3. **Purpose** – the yearning to feel like our work has a greater meaning, that it contributes to something bigger than ourselves and makes a positive impact. If you have ever heard a child say, "What's the point in doing this?" or "Why should I?", as much as their reluctance may appear challenging and even trigger an emotional response, it is important to note that they are seeking the purpose and the motivation to complete the activity. There are different ways in which this may be achieved, such as by giving learning topics real-world context (e.g., plan and purchase the ingredients to then bake the cake for maths or write a letter to an MP for something important to them to gain writing skills), or engaging in project-based learning, encompassing a host of topics within them (rather than studying topics in a standalone fashion). Project-based approaches work well with creating a sense of purpose, e.g., planning and executing a community clean-up, an event or a charity fundraiser. Topic work can be linked in easily and it can still include an interesting lead element.

There is research to suggest that internal factors are powerful in driving us to do things like learn. Think about if you were planning a trip away that you might have waited a while to book. It is something you want to do so you will more than likely spend time finding somewhere nice to stay, researching things to do in the area and planning your days to make the best use of your time. Conversely, if there is a large pile of laundry built up at the end of this fabulous trip that you had just been on, you would probably just get it done the quickest way possible (or, if you are like me, avoid unpacking for a few days, then avoid the laundry for a few more until the time comes that you absolutely have to do it). It is the difference between something you want to do versus something you have to do.

It is also worth noting that intrinsic motivation is within us all. It is pre-programmed and not something that needs to be learned. The key to unlocking it is as simple as doing things that interest us. That's it. There is no complicated process or science that you need to know other than to follow your interests. For the child, allow them to follow their interests.

EXTRINSIC MOTIVATION

The extrinsic value of learning refers to the external benefits or rewards gained from the learning process. These rewards can be tangible, like a good grade, a sticker or payment (in the context of a job), or intangible, like social recognition. While intrinsic value focuses on the inherent joy of learning, extrinsic value focuses on the external motivations that can push someone to learn. Our world is made up of extrinsic motivation to get us to do things. The most obvious is that when we work, we get paid. We need money to survive, so this conditions us to work, as we need to survive.

Here's a deeper look at extrinsic motivation:

Motivation:

- **Goal-Oriented:** Children who are driven by extrinsic value are often motivated by external goals, such as a physical reward for finishing their work, getting good grades, gaining entry into further education or landing a desired job. This can be a powerful motivator, particularly for students who see a clear connection between their learning and their future goals.
- **Focus on Achievement:** Emphasis is often placed on achieving specific outcomes, like high test scores or completing tasks flawlessly. This can help develop a strong work ethic and achieve specific goals.

Extrinsic motivation is a quick way of creating a drive in the learner to complete an activity. Behaviourist approaches rely heavily on extrinsic motivators like rewards and sanctions. The emphasis is on shaping desired behaviours and achieving specific learning outcomes. While this approach can be effective for managing behaviour and promoting rote memorisation, a "love of learning" is less important as the primary objective is to get from A to B. Students might learn simply to get a good grade or avoid punishment, not because they have a genuine interest in the subject matter. Therefore, the behaviourist approach can be less effective in promoting long-term knowledge retention, critical thinking skills and intrinsic motivation for learning.

Within a therapeutic approach to education, the emphasis moves away from external rewards and punishments (extrinsic motivators) and towards fostering a love of learning for its inherent value (intrinsic motivation). This aligns with the therapeutic goal of building self-esteem and a positive self-image. By acknowledging effort, celebrating progress and highlighting a student's unique strengths, we can create a safe and supportive environment. In this environment, students feel comfortable taking risks, exploring new ideas and experiencing the inherent joy of discovery. This intrinsic motivation becomes the driving force behind learning, fostering a sense of accomplishment and a lifelong love of knowledge.

While behaviourism, perennialism and essentialism all have a focus on extrinsic motivation, constructivism, progressivism and existentialism all prioritise intrinsic motivation. Students are encouraged to construct their own understanding through active exploration and problem-solving. These are all student-centred approaches and focus on the learning process itself, not just the result. The teacher (or the educator) acts as a facilitator, guiding children to make connections between new information and their existing knowledge. This fosters a sense of agency and ownership over learning, leading to a deeper understanding and a more intrinsic desire to explore and learn. However, unlike the therapeutic approach which prioritises emotional well-being, constructivism primarily focuses on cognitive development and knowledge construction.

What we see here with intrinsic and extrinsic motivation is that there is a place for both of them. Other therapeutic educators would argue that intrinsic motivation is more powerful in the long term than extrinsic motivation, but I believe there is a place for both. Ultimately, our children will turn into the next generation of workers and entrepreneurs, and they have to understand how to push themselves to get what they want. Understanding what drives them will help with this motivation as they get older.

INTEREST-LED LEARNING

Harnessing a child's natural curiosity and intrinsic motivation can create an engaging and effective learning experience.

One of the challenges with a behaviourist approach to learning is that much of the motivation to learn is extrinsic. It's all about the reward, whether this is a sticker, school points or the incentive to move to the next stage in learning. Whilst this will motivate most for a short time, it will not work in the long term and it does not work for everyone. The motivating factor can quickly get old if the reward is the same every time. There is also less scope for an interest-led approach. As humans, if we are only semi-motivated to do something and there is an extrinsic reward at the end of it, we are likely to do the minimum we need to do to get the reward. In this situation, the child learns a pre-written curriculum that has been mapped out for them and then is tested to see how much knowledge they have retained on the topics. The limiting factors are the fact that extrinsic motivation has been used, i.e., the test and the curriculum are set. There is no motivation to go above and beyond the realms of what needs to be learnt. There is no reward for that and therefore no room for any interest-led learning.

The process, of course, is preparing them to become part of a future workforce – working in return for money as a reward. This is conditioned into them from a very young age, almost as soon as they start school. Creativity is arguably hindered; the approach is very much centred around the teacher or the educating institution and there is little scope for interest-led enquiry unless it falls within the curriculum that they have to learn. Behaviourists might say that creativity is unimportant in learning and the objective is just to get them to learn the curriculum.

Sometimes, this extrinsic motivation strategy can lead to disengagement, reluctance or refusal, which, in a behaviourist approach, become categorised as a behaviour problem, which would then be dealt with using sanctions to try and remove that behaviour.

An interest-led approach is a different way of educating the child. For the strategy to be successful, a relationship with the learner is needed, whereby the educator understands their interests and how the child likes to work. It's important to note that the educator (regardless of whether this is a tutor, teacher or parent) does not act as the one controlling the learning. They are facilitating learning that the child wants to do. Interest-led learning usually comes from a question from the child regarding something they are curious about.

For example, perhaps a child is interested in gardening but will do little else. The educator could use this information to create opportunities to gain real-life experiences of growing things inside and outside and create resources to help them learn, in the context of gardening, for all their curriculum topics. This would allow the learner to embrace an interest of theirs and engage in the necessary learning at the same time. Using this project-based approach strategy also allows for more holistic learning to take place, rather than standalone subjects – for example, gardening could include S.T.E.M-based learning, such as learning about hydroponic systems, horticulture, farming, maths (in planning space needed to plant things or projecting crop quantities). In essence, it would cover all the topics without the child needing to sit down for formal learning.

Alternatively, if there is content that the child needs to be taught for one reason or another (such as language acquisition or mathematics), then the educator can use information that they know about the child to create content which links with their interests.

For example, if there was a child who did not enjoy doing maths and was always disengaged with the subject, but the educator knew that they were interested in animals, they could use this to help the child do mathematical work and provide a real-life context. For example, they could do a study on the population of red and grey squirrels in the UK. This could even be linked with real-life experiences, visiting an area where there are squirrels, creating tally charts and then handling that data in various ways to acquire mathematical skills. The child would be far more likely to be engaged because this was a real-life scenario in which they were interested, and it would not necessarily feel like a traditional maths worksheet being presented to them in a school setting. This suggests that it is the experience of maths that they previously didn't enjoy, rather than the subject itself. Presented this way, within a topic of interest, they may not even realise that they were doing it

One of the huge benefits of interest-led is that it does not limit how much the child can learn while they are engaged in a particular topic. It takes an interest, provides some structure around it through support from the facilitator and then lets the child pursue their curiosity to whatever level they want to or are able to. It also creates an opportunity for the child to consider what their interests actually are. It gets them looking at the world differently and asking questions based on what they find. Arguably, it creates deeper learning and more inquiry-based thinking within the child, too.

The challenges of interest-led, of course, are that there are not enough resources within a mainstream schooling system to roll it out in mass. It will require a massive thinking shift in the entire system and a change to the way education is brought about. To get to know every child and to pursue an interest-based route for each of them would be a mammoth task. It would require more resources within the system than are currently available. Educators need to be far more highly trained as well and have a really deep understanding of student-centred learning – enough that they could take a more hands-off approach and act as facilitators.

Currently, the approach is centred around the educator/institution. A shift would mean that it would be more difficult to measure progress if children were all pursuing interest-based learning. It would have to be okay that progress is not measured in the same way that it is now. Thinking a bit further, the entire country would have to shift, because no longer would GCSE results or the highest level of education be the most important or determining factors of whether a child was capable of doing a particular job. It would be more passion-based, and the prospective employer would potentially need to take the time to find out more about what drives a member of staff rather than looking at numerical data on a CV. Arguably though, they would get a much more passionate employee, with a genuine interest in the job. This then begs the following questions: for the institution as it currently is, does this assume that the measuring of progress is more important than the learning aspect itself? And is it truly the most beneficial to the learner?

Is it really the case that the behaviourist approach is set up to create an average learner who can do an average job rather than excellence in anything in particular? An interest-led route has a focus on things that are intrinsic and create passion. Behaviourism doesn't allow us to look at these things because they are not observable, so we may be living in a world where the bigger system will never change.

If a child has an opportunity to experience lead learning, whether through home education or otherwise, the child has been truly fortunate because they have been able to experience something that most children do not.

UNLOCKING CURIOSITY

When children are young, they are naturally curious and they ask lots of questions about the world around them. Unfortunately, many eventually unlearn this or become more reluctant to ask their questions as they get older because they are told to not ask questions or are silenced by adults. Sometimes they are instructed to "do as they are told" and encouraged not to ask questions. In some cultures, there are still attitudes that children should be seen and not heard, which is enforced through conditioning too.

Regardless of why this happens, the result is that the child is already becoming accustomed to a behaviourist approach – to follow instructions, do as they are told and not question things. This can be damaging to learning and curiosity.

That said, it is not all bad news! Luckily we are all predisposed to being curious and playing to learn. It is not something we need to be taught. Curiosity is within us all and can be a really powerful tool in learning. The question "Why?" is the fuel that propels learning. It creates that initial curiosity and interest. It is something that should never be unlearned. Children should be encouraged to ask more questions, not fewer!

Every question asked (and answered) is more learning achieved. Curiosity is an urge to understand. It is the driving force behind a love of learning and a potential future passion. It can also be contagious. For example, if you are taking a walk and you stop to look very closely at something around you (it could be a flower, a hole in the ground or anything really), the chances are that whoever you are walking with will also become curious and start to look at it as well, to help you gain an understanding of the answers you are seeking. This, in itself, can be a powerful way to get a child engaged in learning without them realising that they are doing so.

Curiosity is also the difference between textbook learning to gain some basic understanding of a topic, and a deeper understanding with genuine interest in the subject. Studies show curious children tend to perform better in school too.

So, how can we foster more curiosity within a learning setting (regardless of the approach/ philosophy that we are using)? The more everyday tasks that we can turn into explorations and real-world experiences, the more curiosity we can invoke. Asking open-ended questions alongside these experiences makes it even more interesting.

Child: "Why is the sky blue?"

Educator: "Why do you think?"

Child: "I don't know"

Educator: "How do you think we might find out?"

Following their curiosity with questions and then a collaborative approach to get the answer not only allows for interest-based learning but also gives them strategies for learning independently, so they know how to find answers to their questions too. This will eventually turn into a lifelong skill.

Remember that curiosity is fuelled by drive and motivation too. A meaningful relationship with the learner will help to know what drives them. Intrinsic and extrinsic motivation are important here.

Examples include (but are not limited to) physically having the experience of doing something rather than reading about it, science experiments to simulate things or visiting places and making observations. Videos can help if the physical experience is not possible but should be used as a secondary tool rather than the main way of showing things. Project-based approaches to learning create a wider sense of purpose and allow for topics that are seemingly unrelated to one another the opportunity to connect in unexpected ways.

Once you start to explore a topic and an interest is sparked, you may find yourself wandering off into "rabbit holes" or tangents that you did not initially plan for. This is okay. Lean into it, it's usually where some of the best learning happens! Don't be afraid of not knowing all the answers. You can explore and learn together. Learning will become more collaborative and feel less like structured learning. That is okay too!

LEARNING THROUGH PLAY

This is something that is so very underrated. Learning through play is effective for both children and adults. Playful exploration enables independence of thought, invokes curiosity and creates huge engagement. Why are things like game shows so popular on TV, or a competition or a quiz so attractive? Why do newspapers still contain an entire page of crossword puzzles, sudoku and other similar games at the back? Our brains LOVE games, puzzles and hands-on play. It makes us feel calm and relaxes us.

Some of the other things that play can provide us with (aside from fun and enjoyment) include mastery and achievement (think intrinsic motivation!), social connection, exploration and discovery, and fulfilling fantasies and identities. If we then take it a step further and find ways to connect learning to play-based learning, it can only be a winning combination!

The science behind play-based learning is also compelling and highlights the importance of play for a child's development. Play stimulates the growth of new neurons inside our brains and strengthens synapses in those brain regions crucial for learning, memory and problem-solving. In other words, play alters our brain and helps to build it! Studies even suggest play deprivation can negatively impact brain development. Let's not forget that we are all predisposed to learning through play too! There was a time when schools did not exist. Humans still survived and had the ability to learn what they needed to do in order to do so. From a young age, play was how they did this. As a species, we have not changed. Play is still the number one way our brains like to absorb information.

Through play, children experiment, explore cause-and-effect relationships and practise critical thinking skills. Roleplay, for example, allows them to imagine scenarios and test solutions, helping them to be more creative and innovative. It is also a natural training ground for social interaction. Children learn to cooperate, take turns, communicate effectively and resolve conflicts. They also develop empathy and emotional regulation by navigating social situations during play.

SOURCES:

Learning through Play: A framework for policy and practice:
https://research.acer.edu.au/learning_processes/33/

Learning through Play: What the Science says:
https://learningthroughplay.com/explore-the-research/the-scientific-case-for-learning-through-play

CHAPTER SEVEN

RELUCTANCE TO LEARNING

It is not always plain sailing with learning. Reluctance is something we all display at various points in our lives. Children of all ages can demonstrate reluctance to learn at the best of times too. Reluctance can be challenging and draining at times but try not to end up battling with the child and locking heads over them not wanting to do whatever the task is.

If you are working with a therapeutic approach in mind, some strategies can help with reducing reluctance and thereby getting a more positive attitude from the child when you approach a learning activity with them. One of the most important things to remember is that the behaviour that they are displaying when they are showing reluctance is only important to understand the root of the reluctance. Why they are displaying that behaviour is so much more significant in dealing with any kind of reluctant behaviour.

Dealt with in this way, you are far more likely to get a longer-lasting result than dealing with reluctance using a behaviourist approach of sanctioning the behaviour that you see in the moment.

WHY MIGHT RELUCTANCE OCCUR?

Let's think about reasons why they may be refusing to do a learning activity.

FEAR OF FAILURE

There may be a fear of failure or a fear of the unknown. This could particularly be the case if they have had failure messages in the past from a school environment where they were unable to succeed in the task that you were trying to get them to do.

SEN NEED

If the child has a special educational need, for example, autism, ADHD or PDA, they will likely need certain strategies to support them to learn. They will struggle to engage with any kind of learning that is not presented to them with these access strategies in mind.

SENSORY NEED

Some children, especially those who have special educational needs, also have sensory needs or may have a sensory processing disorder. Sensory needs can include things like the desire to touch things, the feeling of not wanting to be touched, needing to be hugged or compressed, low noise, the need to move constantly, the need for less visual stimulation or various things in between. Sensory needs can be a plethora of different things and you'd be surprised how quirky some needs can be.

FATIGUE

It may sound obvious, but things like not sleeping enough and therefore being tired, not having enough breakfast and therefore being hungry or just having a bit of a cold and being unwell are all examples of things that might create reluctance to learning. Even adults feel this. If we are not feeling 100% ourselves then it's really hard to engage with other activities. Think about Maslow's hierarchy of needs.

BOREDOM/DISLIKE OF THE TOPIC

If the child is not interested in a topic or feels bored because they have overworked in an area at any given time, they may feel like they can't be bothered to do any more. It is no longer an area of interest at that time.

EMOTIONAL ISSUES

Have they recently been through educational trauma? Are there any negative emotions affecting them at the moment like sadness, anger or frustration? No self-confidence, nervousness about trying something new and stubbornness are all things that fall into this category, too.

EXTERNAL FACTORS

Things that might happen in the world around them may make them feel more reluctant to do any learning. Losing a loved one, grieving over a pet, something that is happening in the news or in the local area or other things that might be going on at home can all be factors that affect their willingness to learn.

If it is boredom or dislike of the topic, they have lost intrinsic motivation to continue. They no longer feel the drive to do so. This is why interest-led learning is so important. There are different ways to approach this. With core topics that you might want them to learn, such as English and maths, you can embed it into project-based learning so that they are not sitting down and doing standalone English or maths. If it is topical learning that they have become bored of, consider the level of challenge. Was it too easy or hard for them? If not, perhaps they have just lost interest. Leave it alone and come back to it another time.

Whatever the physical display of reluctance might look like, there are three categories to which the reluctance can belong: behavioural reluctance, emotional reluctance and physical reluctance. Sometimes, they may refuse because of a combination of the different categories. Emotional reluctance is almost always included as part of one of the other two.

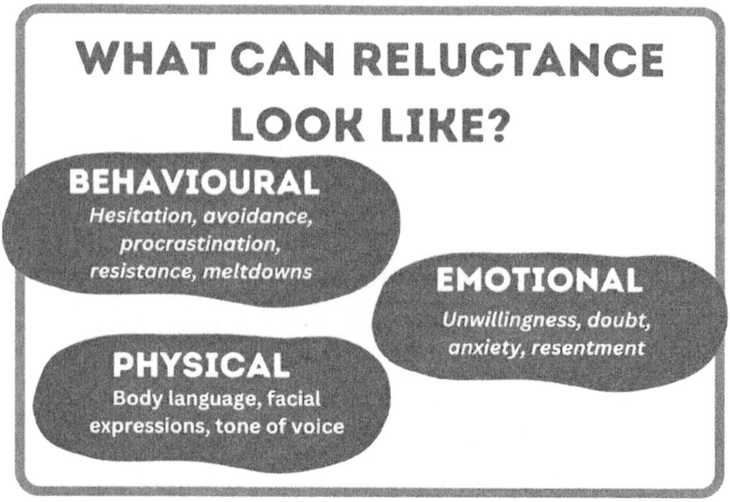

Behavioural reluctance is about what they are doing to be reluctant. Defiance, arguments, tantrums, meltdowns, unproductive behaviour, procrastination and avoidance are all very common in behavioural reluctance.

Emotional reluctance is more about their feelings. There are feelings attached to almost everything we do so this will always play a part in whatever it is they are refusing to do. Any kind of negative emotion will play its part in refusal or reluctance to do an activity.

Physical reluctance has more to do with the body itself. Things like tiredness or fatigue, pain or discomfort, illness or perhaps they are stretching themselves in a sporting activity that they want to get better at or playing a musical instrument, for example, where their fingers may ache as they start to pick up pace while learning to play.

DIFFERENT SORTS OF RELUCTANCE

Before you start to deal with any kind of reluctance therapeutically, take some time to think about which category it falls into (or which combination of categories). To be able to do this, you need to think about why they are displaying certain behaviours rather than what it is you are seeing.

What sort of reluctance is it and what behaviour is the child displaying? This information is vital to dealing with it effectively and alleviating it entirely in the future as well. Here is some helpful guidance on what you can do with a different kind of reluctance that you might experience.

Emotional Reluctance

- Identify the emotion: Pinpoint the specific emotion (fear, anxiety, sadness, etc.)
- Challenge negative thoughts
- Build confidence by referring to past successes
- Practice relaxation techniques

Behavioural Reluctance

- Break down tasks
- Use rewards (Intrinsic/ Extrinsic)
- Time management
- Realistic expectations – meet them where they are at and set realistic goals from there

Physical Reluctance

- Gradual increase- e.g. with sport or learning a new skill like ballet
- Rest and recovery
- Ensure adequate sleep and nutrition to support physical energy.

DEALING WITH RELUCTANCE

Using the information above and the following steps will help you to deal with reluctance therapeutically, create a happier learning environment and give you both strategies for success going forward.

Make observations of how reluctance is being displayed.

1. Look at what you are physically seeing when they refuse. Are they having a meltdown? Do they think they can't do it? Do they look stressed?
2. What are they saying and how are they saying it? Is their tone of voice angry, disaffected or bored?
3. How are they feeling? Are there any emotions that you can pick up from their body language?

Try Identifying the cause. Why is the child refusing?

1. Consider some of the things we talked about earlier, e.g., fear of failure and SEN needs.
2. Observe if the child displays reluctance to learning in general, or if it is a specific type of activity. There may be something you have not thought of or they have not shared with you yet. For example, they may hate writing and have a meltdown when you ask them to put pen to paper, but the underlying reason could be something like:
    a) their fingers hurt when they hold the pen in position
    b) they struggle with spelling (possible dyslexia)

c) a previous trauma such as another child telling them they had messy handwriting in the past
d) they don't like the sound of the pencil writing on the paper.

The list is endless.

Offer choices/alternative options.

1. Try and give them something that they can have some control over to help motivate them. For example, the time of day that they do the task, the environment (e.g., build a den and do the work there), what stationary they use etc.
2. Meet them where they are at. Have realistic expectations of what they can/ will achieve. For example, if you want them to write an essay and they want to do nothing, perhaps you could offer them a negotiation. They could do a paragraph, or they can use speech-to-text to "write" it on an electronic device, or they can spend some time doing what they want to do now and agree on a time at which they will come back to the essay.
3. Connect learning to their interests. You will always get more participation if activities and learning are interest-based and have a bigger context. For example, with maths, looking out of the window and creating a tally chart of all the colours of all the cars that drive by for an hour and then graphing that up is so much more fun than doing a worksheet on statistics.
4. Motivation is key, so know what makes them tick. What drives them? Interest-based learning will always be good for intrinsic motivation. You can always stick in a few extrinsic motivation rewards if you think they will go for them as well.

Set them up to succeed!

1. Create a positive learning environment (safe, supportive, free of anxiety)
2. Be a good role model
3. Praise their efforts

CHAPTER EIGHT

THE ART OF RELAXATION

Let's start this chapter by taking a deep breath. A deep breath to relax, take it easy and accept the imperfections in our lives. Nobody has the perfect life and there are no children anywhere, ever, Neurotypical or otherwise, that always do exactly what you think they are going to do at exactly the time you think they are going to.

Instead of battling with the quirks and things that are not perceived as social norms, in this chapter, we are going to learn to lean into those things, the differences, and celebrate the big wins that they bring us.

We live in a world where children feel pressure to achieve from a very young age. They compare themselves to the other children around them and if they have ever entered mainstream schooling, education (and fun) is quantified from very early on – spelling tests, performances and even competitive sports. As they get older, this becomes more about things like how many GCSEs they will get or how qualified they are for the next stage they want to get to in life.

While it is great that some things can be quantified in this way, it takes away from the fun aspect of learning and makes it more about all that is needed for the next stage. It is also very unnecessary. This approach does not suit everyone, and education should not feel like it is linear. Most career paths have multiple avenues into them and one path is no more superior than another.

There is also a lot to be said for enjoying one's childhood and embracing learning things you are interested in. I've said it more than once in this book; we are predisposed to learn. Children learn through play. Adults even learn through play! We are all naturally curious and we will find a way to get there. In other words, they don't have to know what they want to be when they grow up at any age. Even when they are a grown-up, they have choices if they want to try out different things. All they really have to do is follow their passions and continue to do so into adulthood. The rest will come. It is as simple as that.

For example, if a child realised that they were into archaeology as they were growing and decided to make a career of it, they would eventually figure out what qualifications they needed or how they could enter into that profession and work their way into it. There are very few careers that have a rigid path that you have to take from a very young age to be able to get into them.

PERFECTION IS MYTH

Have you ever heard the saying "Beauty is in the eye of the beholder"? A similar concept can be applied to perfection.

There is no such thing as "normal" and perfection is merely somebody looking sideways at somebody else and wanting to be more like them. This is lovely, except by looking sideways, you never see the whole picture. Your perception of perfection is an ideal rather than a reality.

Each of us is different and each of us has different strengths and weaknesses. Our differences are something to be admired, not to be compared.

WHY IS RELAXATION IMPORTANT?

Without going into the nitty-gritty of relaxation (we can perhaps save this topic for another day), we can say that relaxation in general has physical, mental and emotional benefits to the body.

It is no coincidence that reluctance (in learning and otherwise) also comes from physical, mental and emotional states that are under stress. This suggests that when a child is not in a relaxed state, or part of them is not feeling relaxed, they are not ready to learn. They may put barriers in the way or refuse altogether.

Regular relaxation can be used as a preventative technique for future problems. It is an art. It is something that you have to practise all of the time, find strategies that work for you and then make sure that you use them regularly. Many of us wait too long to relax. We wait until we already feel stressed, or mental, physical or emotional damage has already been done to us for one reason or another before we try and find ways to relax. What we should be doing is practicing relaxation techniques all of the time, so that we are more resilient and ready to face challenges when they are presented to us in various aspects of our lives.

Starting to practise these techniques young is wonderful for our overall lives and can only enhance our educational experiences too. It does not have to be big things either. A series of small changes that children build into their lives can make a world of difference and act as a genuine support strategy within itself.

RELAXATION TOOLS TO SUPPORT LEARNING

Support strategies are commonly used with children who access an alternative provision or have special educational needs. However, they are a brilliant tool for all children (and adults). Here are a few ideas of things you can try. It is important to note that you don't need to do all of them. Just pick one or two to start with and see if they work. Try to do them regularly so that they become part of a routine.

MOVEMENT BREAKS

These are a great way to refocus the brain after a bout of learning and concentration. They allow for a release of physical energy. Some studies show that short bursts of physical activity can increase blood flow to the brain, leading to improved focus, attention and memory. It does not need to be long. Just a few minutes every thirty to sixty minutes can help to get them learning more effectively.

Stress and frustration are common in learning. When acquiring a new skill, it doesn't always go the way you plan the first time around and sometimes requires a little bit of perseverance. Adding movement breaks can help combat some of the stress and frustration. The release of endorphins can help boost the mood and help the learner feel a sense of calm once again. They can be added into an everyday routine for learners who like a bit more structure and even gamified. For example, half past every hour is movement break time each day, or every time they hear you say a certain word, they have to get up and run around waving their hands for ten seconds. Strategies like this can help to reduce disruption or reluctance because the learner knows that movement has been planned into their day and they won't be sat doing an activity for too long.

TIMERS

These can be quite useful during sessions of learning. These could be digital or manual. Sand timers work well for visual learners. Sometimes children struggle to visualise what a period of time looks like. If they can physically see this on the sand timer and know that they only have so long to complete an activity, or until the next break, this helps them to visualise how much time they have. It can also help them with the transition to the next thing.

Timers can be powerful tools used therapeutically during learning in several ways:

- **The Pomodoro Technique:** This method uses a timer to break down work into focused intervals (usually twenty-five minutes) separated by short breaks (typically five minutes). This helps with concentration and prevents burnout, especially for learners who struggle with staying on task.
- **Timed Activities:** Set a timer for specific tasks like reading, writing or completing problems. This helps learners stay on track and avoid procrastination. It can also be motivating to "beat the clock" and finish the task before the timer goes off.
- **Transition Timers:** Use a timer to signal the end of an activity and give a gentle reminder to prepare for the next one. This helps with transitions, which can be challenging for some learners.
- **"Work Until" Timer:** Flip the traditional timer concept. Set a timer for a short, focused work period, letting the learner know they can take a break once the timer goes off. This can be motivating, especially for tasks that might seem tedious.
- **Reward Breaks:** you can pair a timer with a short reward break. Set a timer for a focused work period and after it goes off, the learner gets a short break to do something they enjoy. This can be particularly helpful for learners who need frequent reinforcement to stay on track.

DEEP BREATHING EXERCISES

Pair a timer with deep breathing exercises. Set the timer for a few minutes and guide the learner to focus on slow, controlled breaths. This can be particularly helpful for learners who experience anxiety or difficulty calming down.

MINDFULNESS BREAKS

Similar to deep breathing, set a timer for a short mindfulness break. This could involve guided visualisation or simply focusing on bodily sensations. Timers help ensure the break doesn't become too long and disrupt the learning flow.

Remember, there is no right or wrong answer here and it is likely that the strategies you use will change as your child grows and develops. Observing their learning style and using success strategies together with a nurturing environment and purposeful learning spaces are the perfect ingredients for engaged and deep learning experiences. There are an infinite number of ways to achieve this.

CHAPTER NINE

THE PROBLEM AND THE SOLUTION

There are some huge challenges in the education system at present. Inclusion and accessibility play a part in that. It isn't that the people within the system don't care, but more because the system was set up to provide a service years ago and very little has changed since then. It is delivered in the same way it always has been. The thought process is that most children will be able to access it in the way that it currently is and learn something. The enjoyment of education is not a factor used to measure its success as it currently is because this is not an observable behaviour.

The mainstream education system is organised with a process, where learning is monitored through observation. progress is measurable, meaning learning can be quantified and compared and analysed statistically, before moving them along to the next thing in their lives.

The education institution is a behaviourist system, for the most part. In other words, only observable behaviours are used to measure progress. Naturally, this means that non-observable behaviours, such as mental health needs, invisible disabilities or SEN, are not taken into consideration when measuring progress or giving sanctions for not meeting targets. There is an awareness of the necessity of this, because pastoral services do exist, even if there has not been enough of this in the last years.

The challenge comes where all children are expected to make the same amount of progress, regardless of whether they are able to access the curriculum as it currently is. If they can't access it, they are seen as the problem, rather than the system itself. This is one of the biggest reasons for school refusal and children falling out of the mainstream education system in this country at present.

Families home educating because they wish to travel, teach a different way for the pleasure of it or because they follow a particular way of life or faith are now in the minority. More and more families that are electively home-educating now are doing so because they felt they had no other choice, or in some cases have been steered to it because the school could not meet the needs of the child.

Their child did not fit the mainstream system and has suffered educational trauma from the fight they had to endure with the institution, or they do not believe that their child would be able to access it from the outset and have therefore never attempted to send them as it would be seen as setting them up to fail.

There are not enough alternative provisions. There are hundreds of thousands of children across the country waiting for an alternative provision that doesn't even exist yet, and there is no telling if it ever will.

Furthermore, there need to be more conversations happening nationally that there are more approaches to education philosophies that underpin deep learning than just behaviourist. Everyone- schools, families, alternative provisions and anything in between would benefit from really seeing that there are different ways in which we can educate our young people. Project-based and interest-led learning is far more powerful and provides intrinsic motivation for excellence. They can take a disengaged child who believes that they are a failure and transform them into a happy, creative and enthusiastic child with a very real love of learning that will last a lifetime.

This is what I have seen over the last twenty years. Having started my career as a mainstream teacher, moved up the ranks over the years, then into special education and then launched a company working with those children who are unable to access any kind of education system at all, I have seen education from every angle and found a way to be able to facilitate recognised, certified learning in mass and create true engagement from it at the same time.

Little Crafters Boxes was a craft subscription box company that launched amidst the pandemic and took off like a rocket. All the children were at home at that time as schools were closed. We sold 100 subscription boxes almost as soon as we opened the virtual doors (and then closed the doors again quickly because I got scared of how I was going to fulfil all these orders from what was a glorified shed I had set up for my early retirement in the back garden, having had left teaching). My self-employed joiner husband stopped his day job to help me for a month and four years later, he has still not gone back to his day job yet!

We sold the house and moved to Lincolnshire, where we now occupy a large premises in the countryside. The company still designs, manufactures and distributes boxes from the workshop each month and has evolved to create its child company, LCB Education.

LCB Education offers certified learning opportunities and accredited certification to children and adults, using a combination of constructivism and progressivism, with me and my remote teacher team as the facilitators of the learning opportunities that are offered by the company every month.

It is a child-centred approach. Children can access the AQA unit award scheme and the Children's University, which both offer an alternative approach to recognition of learning. LCB children can access online lessons (short interactive ones on demand) and workbooks as well if they would like some written content. In a nutshell, a combination of resources are available to them to access, each leading to a path of certification. A project-based, interest-led approach, with STEM subjects at the very heart, that they are free to choose from every single month means that they have a choice in the things that they want to learn with a little bit of structure.

Learning in this way is still collaborative. The project has proven that a student-led approach can work in mass numbers with just some small changes to its approach. There are over a thousand children currently accessing this. Most of these children were deemed failures by the behaviourist system they were once in. Now, they love their lives and are achieving again.

The transformation stories are more significant than anything I ever saw in my teaching career. The parents have been so enthused by the approach that many of them have now registered to learn with us, too!

The company has grown exponentially but is still small in the scheme of things. It currently employs ten staff and has been a lovely whirlwind. It is a therapeutic, hands-on, project-based, interest-led learning through play, with an engaged online community and the children at its heart. It's not just the children who have been significant in the development of the company. It's the parents too.

On a personal note, I believe that the success of the company so far is because I listened intently to the needs of entire families and acted upon that (and continue to do so) as I went along. I have pushed boundaries with awarding bodies and the availability of resources in one space, to open doors that were not an option for them before and trial things that I did not see exist in the industry before. Not everything I have done has worked but for the things that have, the impact has been immense. It is not just that the children are engaged in learning again, but also the parents who have breathed a sigh of relief because they have someone to hold their hand on their journey and give them everything they need to help their child move forward.

This is what progress should look like if we were ever going to measure it.

At every stage, the process is thought out to make it therapeutic, educational and progressive. The materials that are used for the crafts are eco-friendly. This, in itself, provides some education for children and normalises the use of sustainable materials. Wood is therapeutic to touch and is one of the main materials that we use. This provides a calming experience while the children are crafting.

There are three difficulty levels for the boxes. This allows children to grow with them and swap and change, depending on their interests and ability level. It also provides an element of choice every single month so that they can be involved in decisions around their interests and the learning that they wish to do in the future.

There is a different learning theme every month, with subcategories in every area of STEAM (science, technology, engineering, arts and maths). The learning themes are chosen by the children in an annual competition – they put their ideas into a virtual hat and then a group of them are invited to HQ to pick their favourites. This helps them have complete control over their learning and they see it as less of a demand if they have had the opportunity to be involved in that decision-making process.

The use of accreditation and the AQA unit award scheme allows children to access structured learning through crafts and learning topics each month. They can choose something that sparks their interest and they have a list of things which they can complete and earn a certificate which recognises what they learned.

This combination of factors and practical strategies to help children engage has had an extraordinary effect on learners and children who were previously struggling to engage.

So, there we have it. This is where we are up to so far.

I will leave you with some words from some of our families to show you the variety of children that are now able to access education, because:

THIS IS ANOTHER WAY

Education has no limits for anyone if there is open-mindedness in its approach. Always look beyond the behaviour and ask why.

> *We needed something self-directed but structured because we were both struggling to find the right balance for us both, adult and child. I couldn't see how LCB and AQA units could possibly work for our PDA neurotype but we gave it a trial and here we still are, nearly a year later and infinitely happier with our learning time.*
>
> — **Stacey Matheson**

> *When we first started home education, none of us could get out of the school mindset of sitting down and working for a set number of hours, which we all struggled with. We have found that since discovering Little Crafters Boxes, we are all more relaxed and able to take a simpler, easier approach to education that has allowed my boys to progress so much more than they were, even the ones not doing AQA.*
>
> — **Michelle Williams**

When we started home educating, I was completely overwhelmed! I was trying to do school at home (because I didn't know any other way) and had two children who were trying to show me that it didn't work for them. I eventually got the message and started to look for other ways to help them learn but was then completely overwhelmed by the number of different resources, curriculums and topics that were available, I was still focusing on reading and writing because that's what everyone says your children need to know by a certain age (even though my daughter was refusing to even look at a book at that point), I eventually found Little Crafters Boxes and joined. In the year since I joined, I've completely changed my education outlook and it now meets the needs of all of my children and us, as a family. As a result, I have relaxed and I absolutely love the education my children are getting now. We learn together happily, through lots of play and experiences, rather than sitting at a table memorising information for tests. My children are learning so much and my daughter, who wouldn't even look at a book, now loves to read.

— Tiffany Fletcher

When we started home education, I seriously doubted myself and my abilities. I just needed Dylan to get through each day. We tried different things, finding a rhythm in making meals, mindfulness and introducing self-care Saturday. Our biggest turning point was finding LCB and AQA UAS. The spark came back, his confidence grew and his self-esteem is higher than it's ever been. Now he's just smashed a mini target of 300 AQAs, completed a level 2 food hygiene certificate and recently helped our neighbour through a panic attack.

— Stacey Marshall

When starting home education, Luke and I were at another level of learning and I doubted if I could give Luke the education he needed. We have had good days and bad days but together we have now set at semi-structured and child-led learning, including everything from cooking to building, to helping others, to art, to coping in the community and joining groups. We have also found Little Crafter Boxes, which I never thought Luke could cope with but he has grown in confidence, wanting to learn new things. He takes an interest in recycling from boxes with his ideas and achieving AQA certificates and passes. Now, going into the second year of LCB, it's going to be another big adventure of joy for Luke. I know two years of home education is the best decision I have made for Luke and he's happy.

— Lisa Evans

We needed hope and a chance. We had a child in full breakdown and the rest of us followed. With the help of the team who gave an accessible education, and an understanding from the whole team, we are on our way to rebuilding. The smile I feared was lost is back on my child's face.

— Laura McNally

When we started our home Ed journey, I had no idea which way to turn. Was this the right decision? I was worried I was going to fail her and her education. I felt so alone as we knew nobody else on the home education journey. THEN, one night, I was scrolling on social media. It was silly o'clock and I was trying to find ways to help support Nevaeh. I came across Little Crafters Boxes. I think it was fate. I read all the comments on the website and then attended the week of lives in an event that the company had put on to support parents who were embarking on this journey.

The fear of being alone on this journey just went. The feeling I was going to fail Nevaeh in her education just disappeared. I think I've bought everything on the website. Nevaeh sat in on some of the lives and sat with me as I went through bits on the pages and website and saw that sparkle and urge to learn again – she was on a countdown to when we could register.

All that from a child who has struggled with learning, not just because she's dyslexic and has autism and was historically working below where she "should" be, speaks volumes to me. We have been made so welcome into the LCB family/community and nothing is too much trouble. I just wish I had found it all sooner but better late than never.

— Natalie Davies Ahearne

ABOUT THE AUTHOR

Radha Borthayre is a former teacher and an educationalist.

After a fifteen year career in teaching (mainstream and special education), during the COVID pandemic, she launched Little Crafters Boxes Ltd. An eco-friendly craft subscription box to support families who were then faced with having children at home for extended periods of time.

Post pandemic, this evolved. The subscription boxes continued. People loved having hands-on projects that the whole family could get involved with and were reporting that their children were finding them fun and therapeutic to do. They were engaging in learning in a new way! The education landscape had also changed. Many children did not return to school, and the world started to look a little bit different.

Radha's passion for education, and to make learning more accessible for those who needed a different way of learning started to resurface and started a sequence of events that would mean the launch of LCB education (a new branch of Little Crafters Boxes). A different way of learning for those who found themselves in the "gap" where they couldn't quite get on with mainstream education but, did not yet have access to alternative provision either.

As she saw how great the need was, she started to develop this further within the company. A new vision to offer accredited hands-on learning, with certification and access to remote testing, and still interest led! Everything the child needed in one place, with a student- centred philosophy at its heart and support community for the whole family. The families involved back then called it "LCB magic".

This is very much still a journey for Radha. The vision for LCB Education is for every child to have access to learning in a way that works for them, and for all the gaps in the education system that exist to be filled with smiley faces and happy learners, whatever education looks like for them (at home or otherwise).

Radha, herself, was born and raised in Leicester, commenced her teaching career in Coventry in her early twenties. This continues in a special educational provision in Rutland for the final decade of her establishment-based teaching practice. She now has two young children and shares her time between rural Lincolnshire, where she lives, and the South of France, where she has extended family.

Radha Borthayre
LCB Education
www.lcbeducation.co.uk

Little Crafters Boxes
www.littlecraftersboxes.co.uk
Atlas House, Westcliffe, Sleaford, Lincolnshire, NG34 8RG

Little Crafters Boxes | Facebook
https://www.facebook.com/groups/littlecraftersboxes

LCB Education | Facebook
https://www.facebook.com/groups/lcbeducation

Printed in Great Britain
by Amazon

60930290R00070